LIFE

OF

CHARLES T. WALKER, D. D.,

("THE BLACK SPURGEON.")

PASTOR MT. OLIVET BAPTIST CHURCH, NEW YORK CITY.

BY

SILAS XAVIER FLOYD, A. M.

WITH AN

INTRODUCTION

BY

ROBERT STUART MacARTHUR, D. D.

NEGRO UNIVERSITIES PRESS
NEW YORK

Originally published in 1902
by the National Baptist Publishing Board

Reprinted 1969 by
Negro Universities Press
A Division of Greenwood Press, Inc.
New York

SBN 8371-2708-4

PRINTED IN UNITED STATES OF AMERICA

DR. CHARLES T. WALKER, 44 YEARS OF AGE.

INTRODUCTION.

There is no species of literary composition more difficult than the writing of a good biography. Biographers are under a great temptation at times to create, or at least to magnify, the virtues of their subjects; and the temptation is not less on other occasions to deny, or greatly to minify, their vices. The biographies of Holy Scripture are models of biographical literary production. Inspired writers neither extenuate the defects nor magnify the excellencies of their subjects; extenuating nothing on the one hand, they do not, on the other, set down aught in malice. The excellence of the inspired writings in this regard differentiates them from the uninspired writings of any country or century.

But while to biographize is a confessedly difficult task, it is at the same time universally admitted to be a form of literary production of great value, when properly executed. A biography is generally understood to be the history of the life, actions and character of a particular person; it is that form of history proper whose subject is described in the facts and events of his individual experience. Carlyle, in his "Sartor Resartus," says: "Biography is by nature the most universally profitable, universally pleasant of all things." He also elsewhere says: "There is no heroic poem in the world but is at bottom a biography, the life of a man." He has frequently expressed the idea that history is biography;

that the history of any nation is the story of the lives of its great men. In a profound sense this statement is literally true. We thus see that peculiar ability is required accurately to write the life of any representative man. His forbears for many generations ought to be accurately known; his environment, in all its essential characteristics, ought to be thoroughly mastered. The times partly make men, and men partly make their time; each acts and reacts upon the other. Neither can be exhaustively described independent of the other.

The difficulty of writing good biographies is so great that comparatively few great biographies have been written. All the world is familiar with the unique biography of Johnson by Boswell. It has excited hearty laughter, while it has imparted valuable information. Lockhart's Life of Scott and Lady Holland's Life of Sydney Smith, fill almost a unique place in biographical literature. G. Otto Trevelyan's Life of Lord Macaulay and Hallam Tennyson's Life of his father are among the more recent and valuable illustrations of the biographical literature of modern times.

The word biography comes from two Greek words, *bios,* life, and *graphein,* to write. In order that there should be a good biography, it is necessary, therefore, that there should be a life nobly lived, and a writer competent to describe it in fitting terms. In the biography of Rev. Charles T. Walker, D. D., by Rev. Silas X. Floyd, D. D., both these conditions are excellently met. By his careful literary training, his wide experience as a writer, and his intimate knowledge of the history of Dr. Walker, Dr. Floyd is eminently fitted to write a readable account of Dr. Walker's life and work. He has been associated in newspaper, pastoral and evangelistic work with Dr. Walker for the past twenty years. When Dr. Walker was business manager of the Augusta Sentinel, Dr. Floyd was its editor; and when Dr. Walker resigned the pastorate of the Tabernacle Baptist Church in Augusta, Ga., Dr. Floyd became his succssor. He thus has had unusual opportunities to study Dr. Walker's public and private life day by day for nearly a quarter of a century. Dr. Floyd is a graduate of Atlanta University, Georgia, from which institution he received the degree of A. M., three years after his graduation. For three years he was employed by the International Sunday School Convention as one of its Field Workers in the South. He is at present in the employ of the American Baptist Publication Society as a Missionary for Georgia and Alabama. The degree of "Doctor of Divinity" was conferred upon him by Morris Brown College, Atlanta, Ga., June 4, 1902.

There is probably no other Negro in the United States, and perhaps no other in the world, who is a better subject for a biography than Charles T. Walker. Many will affirm that Booker T. Washington is the most prominent representative of his race in America; doubtless, in his special department of effort for his people, he is the representatve Negro. But all intelligent men, black or white, familiar with the facts, will say that Dr. Walker is the ablest Negro preacher and pastor in the United States. His racial characteristics are so strongly emphasized that the most bitter opponent of his race cannot attribute his acknowledged ability as thinker, writer and preacher to any interfusion of white blood in his veins. He is a Negro in every drop of his blood. Dr. Walker had careful training as a preparation for the work of the gospel ministry. Too many men, both white and black, rush into the ministry with quite inadequate preparation. The time has come when the apostolic injunction, "Lay hands suddenly on no man," must be literally obeyed. This injunction is especially important in its relation to preachers and pastors of Negro churches. They are the natural and powerful leaders of their people. This is a transition period for the millions of the Negro race in America. Tremendously important racial problems are now demanding solution. Whites and blacks, both North and South, must have great patience with one another in the presence of these pulsing problems. Right solutions will eventually come; and all men must remember that no question is settled truly until it is settled rightly.

Dr. Walker has been an earnest student ever since his school days. He has traveled widely, read extensively and thought profoundly. In all these respects he has set a good example to all preachers and pastors. There is no standing still in professional life. If a man does not advance, he must retrograde; if he does not grow up, he must grow down. Every preacher is like a man on a bicycle—he must go on constantly or go off speedily.

Dr. Walker's ministry in New York has been remarkable for pulpit power and for practical results. His ministry in this city is a distinct accession to the pulpit force of the entire church, irrespective of denominational divisions and creedal distinctions. Perhaps in the entire history of the city no pastor of any church ever had so many accessions to the membership of his church in the same length of time as Dr. Walker has had.

A great future still awaits his ministerial labors. Marvellous possibilities are before his race in America. Booker Washington, Dr. Walker, and a few great Negroes, are wisely training their people for a noble future; they are teaching their people that the time for pitying them, and coddling them, as well as for abusing, not to say lynching, them has passed, never to return. They must take their place as men and women among the men and women of the hour. They are to be neither babied nor bullied; neither petted nor pampered; they ought only to expect and demand simple justice; on their behalf these great leaders demand nothing more, and they will be satisfied with nothing less. To deny them simple justice would be an unspeakable reproach to the dominant race in America. Dr. Walker's greatest days as preacher and pastor are still in the future. That he and his race may worthily perform their whole duty, and grandly attain their high destiny is the sincere desire of every true man, earnest patriot, and devout Christian.

This volume ought to be widely circulated and generally studied. It will give genuine inspiration to all men, white or black, who are struggling for higher and better things for time and eternity. Its general circulation will greatly help the Negro toward the realization of his laudable ambitions as a man, a citizen and a churchman.

ROBERT STUART MACARTHUR.

Study, Cavalry Baptist Church, New York.

DEDICATION.

To
THE YOUNG MEN OF
THE NEGRO RACE IN AMERICA
This Volume
Is Respectfully Dedicated by
THE AUTHOR.

PREFACE.

For the combination of shrewd common sense, fine executive ability, ready speech, genial acceptance of conditions, optimistic faith in the future of his race and self-sacrificing zeal in their behalf, Booker T. Washington stands easily first among the nine million Negroes of America. The greatest claim that has yet been made by the Negro in English Literature, according to the most competent critics, has been made by Paul Laurence Dunbar, who, for the first time in our language, has given literary interpretation of a very artistic completeness to what passes in the hearts and minds of a lowly people. The greatest claim that has been made by the Negro in the field of scholarship has been made by W. E. Burghardt DuBois, Ph. D., the eminent sociologist. But not more certain is it that Washington stands first in the list of Negro educators, and Dunbar first in the list of Negro poets and literary men, and DuBois first among scholars, than that the Rev. Charles T. Walker, D. D., who is popularly called "The Black Spurgeon," stands first among eminent and successful Negro preachers.

Dr. Walker's father died the day before Dr Walker was born His mother died when he was only eight years old. The first seven years of his life he was a slave. Becoming an orphan one year after emancipation, the years of his youth and young manhood were years of great hardship and privation. In this respect, his early life resembled that of other distinguished men of humble origin who have been a power in the world, and whose names have an honorable place on the pages of history. The prophetic reference to Christ, "Though thou be little among the thousands of Judah, yet out of thee shall he come forth unto me that is to be ruler in Israel," has been paralleled in human lives by a host of men whose names and deeds are recorded in history, sacred and profane. From the anointing of the Bethlehemite shepherd boy as King of Israel to the present time, history has furnished innumerable illustrations of the providential selection of men from obscure localities and unpretentious surroundings for great responsibilities and important fields of influence. Again and again, in the history of our own country, we have had memorable examples of men who have left an undying influence, whose early life was without friends, and whose heritage was void of patrimony. Abraham Lincoln, James A. Garfield, Benjamin Franklin, Frederick Douglass, George W. Childs, Henry Wilson, Stephen Girard, Horace Greeley, and a host of others were such men.

One of the most profitable uses of history is the narrative of such lives. Having this in mind, it is safe to say that there is no species of writing of more value than biography. It inspires the young to nobler purposes, develops higher resolves, and proves an incentive to the laudable imitation of men who in prominent positions have proved true to principle and duty. It is in this spirit and with this thought in mind, that I undertake to write the story of the life of Dr. Walker. I confess to a great degree of admiration for the man; I glory in his career; I thought that the story of his life ought to be told; I believe that the telling of his life story will do much to encourage, inspire and incite to new endeavor thousands of young colored men all over the land, who need to be encouraged and inspired, and who, because of the peculiar environments of American civilization, find so little to incite them to high resolves, honest endeavors and upright lives. If, therefore, the story of Dr. Walker's life as told by me shall encourage, inspire or incite one single human being, I shall have my reward.

SILAS XAVIER FLOYD.

Augusta, Ga., February 1, 1902.

THE HOUSE IN WHICH CHARLES T. WALKER WAS BORN. STILL STANDING NEAR HEPHZIBAH, GA.

CONTENTS.

CHAPTER I.

CHAPTER II.

CHAPTER III.

CHAPTER IV.

LIFE OF
CHARLES T. WALKER, D. D.

CHAPTER I.

PARENTAGE AND BIRTH.

It has long been a mooted question as to which State in the Union produces the best class of Negroes. Though there are no scientific data fom which to draw definite conclusions, it is very generally agreed that the best Negroes—the most intellectual, most industrious, wealthiest, and the best behaved Negroes—come either from Virginia or Georgia. If that be true, then, if one is so fortunate as to be a native Georgian with Virginia ancestors, or *vice versa*, he ought to be considered a Negro of superior birth, to say the least. Viewed in this light, Charles Thomas Walker was born to superiority. In 1773, a family of Negroes was brought from Virginia to Burke County, Georgia, by the grandfather of the late Col. A. C. Walker, who was a prominent Georgia planter and politician and who for many years was a member of the Georgia legislature. In 1880, Col. Walker, writing of the Negro Walkers who had descended from the family brought to Georgia by his grandfather, said: "As slaves, they were noted for their admirable qualities, and as freedmen they have sustained their reputa-ition."

Charles Thomas Walker was the fourth in descent from this family. His father was a man of the name of Thomas Walker, and was one of three brothers. Thomas Walker was his master's coachman—a position which only the best and most trustworthy slaves were allowed to hold, and a position which the slaves themselves always considered as a place of honor. The fact, also, that he was a deacon in the church of which he was a member attests the esteem in which he was held by the other slaves. Two of Charles T. Walker's uncles, Joseph T. Walker and Nathan Walker, were both Baptist ministers. The Franklin Covenant Baptist Church, about five miles from Hephzibah, Ga., and only a short distance from the Burke County line, was organized for the colored people in 1848. In 1852 or 1853, this church, though its membership was made up of slaves, raised the necessary amount and purchased the freedom of the Rev. Joseph T. Walker, at that time their pastor, in order that he might devote himself entirely to his church work and to the preaching of the gospel in the counties of Richmond, Jefferson and Burke. In this work, Rev. Joseph T. Walker continued until the close of the war. The Rev. Nathan Walker, though a licensed preacher before the war, was not ordained to the ministry until 1866, when he succeeded his brother as pastor of the Franklin Covenant Baptist Church.

In 1848, Thomas Walker was married to a young woman of the name of Hannah Walker. To them eleven children were born —six females and five males. On the 5th day of February, 1858, near Hephzibah, Richmond County, Ga., about sixteen miles southwest of Augusta, their youngest child—Charles Thomas

Walker—was born. Thomas Walker, the father, was buried the day before Charles was born, having died of pneumonia. Mrs. Hannah Walker survived her husband eight years, dying in Augusta, Ga., in 1866. It is related of her that she was a woman of unusual piety and strength of character, being a devout member of the Franklin Covenant Baptist Church, of which her husband was a deacon. She had high hopes and fond expectations for her youngest child, and longed to live to see him make a great and good man of himself, and especially so, because of the sad death of his father which occurred only two days before the child was born. God willed otherwise, and took her home to be with him and to watch from the "high and uplifted" battlements of glory the career of her son.

The following tribute to Mrs. Hannah Walker is taken from "Under the Stars and Bars; or Memories of Four Years' Service with the Confederate Army." This book was written by Mr. Walter A. Clark, Treasurer of Richmond County, Ga. Mr. Clark was a prominent officer in the Confederate Army; he is a graduate of Emory College (Georgia), and a literary man of great merit; he is a nephew of the late Col. Walker, already quoted in this book, was reared along with the black Walkers and knows whereof he speaks. His tribute to Mrs. Walker is no less a credit to the memory of the deceased than it is a testimony of the goodness of heart and magnificent manhood of the writer.

"My heart prompts me to pay its earnest tribute to one whose memory the sketch above recalls—dear old Aunt Hannah. How her name brings back to my heart and life to-day the glamour of the old, old days that will never come again—days when to me a barefoot boy, life seemed a long and happy holiday! I can see her now, her head crowned with a checkered handkerchief, her arms bare to the elbows, her spectacles set primly on her nose, while from her kindly eyes there shone the light of a pure white soul within! She was only an humble slave, and yet her love for me was scarcely less than that my father and mother bore me; and when, on a summer's day in 1861, my brother and myself left the old homestead to take our humble places under a new born flag, there was not a dry eye on the whole plantation, old Aunt Hannah wept in grief as pure and deep as if the clods were falling on an own child.

"Long years have come and gone since she was laid away in the narrow house appointed for all the living. No marble head-stone marks the spot, yet I am sure the humble mound that lies above her sleeping dust covers a heart as honest and as faithful, as patient and as gentle, as kindly and as true, as any that rests beneath the proudest monument that art could fashion or affection buy. She reared a large family of children, the Rev. Charles T. Walker, 'The Black Spurgeon,' among them, and transmitted to them all a character for honesty and virtue marked even in those the better days of the Republic.

"Wisely or otherwisely, in the order of Providence, or in the order of Napoleon's 'heavier battalions,' we have in this good year of our Lord (1900) not only a New South, but a new type of Aunt Hannah. The old is, I fear, a lost Pleiad, whose light will shine no more on land or sea or sky."

The Walker family produced a number of able and successful preachers—some say more, some say less. As already shown, two of Dr. Walker's uncles—Joseph T. Walker and Nathan Walker—were ministers. The latter is still living, venerated and honored, at the good old age of 85. He was one of the founders of the Walker Baptist Association, and was for more than twenty years its moderator, retiring about ten years ago on account of the infirmities of old age. The Association was named in honor of the Rev. Joseph T. Walker. The Walker Baptist Institute at Augusta, named also for the Rev. Joseph T. Walker, was founded by this Association and has been for many years supported by it. In all respects the Walker Baptist Association is to-day the leading Association in Georgia. An older brother of Dr. Walker, the Rev. Peter Walker, now retired on account of age, was, in his day, a man of great force and power in the pulpit. A nephew of Dr. Walker the Rev. Prof. Joseph A. Walker, son of Rev. Peter Walker, was up to the time of his death, about eight years ago, the honored and successful Principal of Walker Baptist Institute. Besides these, there are two first cousins of Dr. Walker who are among Georgia's most distinguished clergymen—the Rev. W. G. Johnson, D. D., Pastor of the First Baptist Church, Macon, Ga., who is Secretary of the Walker Baptist Association, Chairman of the Board of Trustees of the Walker Baptist Institute, and a member of the Board of Trustees of the Atlanta Baptist College; and the Rev. R. J. Johnson, Pastor of the First Baptist Church, Millen, Ga., and Treasurer of the Board of Trustees of the Walker Baptist Institute. Other cousins in the ministry are the Rev. Samuel C. Walker, Augusta, Ga., Rev. A. J. Walker, Millen, Ga., Rev. T. W. Walker, Wrightsville, Ga., Rev. Solomon Walker, Savannah, Ga., Rev. Matthew Walker, Savannah, Ga., an elder in the C. M. E. Church, and Rev. Nathan

Wilkerson, Waynesboro, Ga. In addition to these, there are many of this family who were once in the ministry of earth, but who have long since gone to join the ministry on high.

Descended from a generation of preachers, Dr .Walker towers above them all like Saul among his brethren. So great is his fame and so celebrated has he made the name of Walker that the other members of the family find it a passport in many places for them to make it known that they belong to the generation of Walkers.

CHAPTER II.

EARLY CHILDHOOD.

The first seven years of young Walker's life were spent under the hard tuition of slavery, though, of course, he cannot have any very vivid recollections of the hardships of those days. It is fair, nevertheless to assume that his lot was not different from that of thousands and thousands of other black children in different parts of the South. Richmond County, one of the large "Black Belt" counties of Georgia, which had then, and which has to this day, a larger black than white population, was in no respect different in its slave customs and regulations from other slave communities, excepting possibly the religious privileges enjoyed by the slaves. They had their own churches and enjoyed for the most part the ministrations of colored preachers, such as they were. They had their own houses of worship, their own church officials, and held regular and stated religious meetings. This was true in only a very limited number of places in the South during the slave period. In this respect, Richmond County was somewhat in advance of other localities. But only in this respect. In other matters, it was the same in Richmond County as elsewhere. The slaves received regular rations or allowances. The monthly ration consisted of eight pounds of pickled pork or its equivalent in fish. The pork was often tainted and the fish of the poorest quality.

With this, they had one bushel of unbolted Indian meal, of which quite fifteen per cent. was fit only for pigs, and one pint of salt. This was the entire monthly allowance for a full grown slave. The children had no regular allowance, and often were compelled to dispute with dogs and cats and pigs over the scraps thrown into the yard or into the swill tub. Children not large enough to work in the field had neither shoes, stockings, jackets nor trousers given them. Their clothing consisted of two coarse tow linen shirts per year, and when these were worn out, they were literally naked until the next allowance day. Flocks of children from five to ten years old might be seen on the plantations as destitute of clothing as any little heathen in Africa, and this even in the cold and dreary months of winter. These children had no school advantages—certainly not. It was made a misdemeanor by law to teach a colored person to read or write. These children had no home life. The night for the slave—male and female—was shortened at both ends. The slaves worked as long as they could see, and were usually up late cooking and mending for the coming day, and at the first gray streak of the morning were summoned to the fields by the driver's horn. Young mothers working in the field were allowed to go home about ten o'clock in the morning to nurse their children. Sometimes they were compelled to take their children with them and leave them in the corners of the fences in order to prevent loss of time. John Wesley, the founder of Methodism, who got his knowledge of slavery while sojourning in the colony of Georgia, did not err when he denounced slavery as "the sum of all villainies."

In such a school as this, Charles Thomas Walker received his early training. How different from the early training of such men as Henry Wilson, Abraham Lincoln, William McKinley, James A. Garfield, Daniel Webster, Henry Clay, and other white men who were born to poverty. Though these men were born in humble circumstances, yet they were born to freedom. Charles Thomas Walker was born poor, and—what was worse—he was born a slave. These men owned at least themselves; they were free to go wherever they desired or to pursue any course of study or line of work that they wished. Charles Thomas Walker owned nothing—not even himself — and was compelled to go wherever his master ordered and do whatever his master commanded.

As to this slave system, the ancient question might well be asked, "Can any good thing come out of Nazareth?" And the reply is,

> "Full many a gem of purest ray serene,
> The dark unfathomed caves of ocean bear;
> Full many a flower is born to blush unseen,
> And waste its sweetness on the desert air."

And how we thank God that we can write of this dreadful system of iniquity in the past tense. It did crush and cower so much of genius and intellectual strength and moral grandeur, and did send to their graves without opportunity and without chance thousands and thousands who, under any just and equitable scheme of civilization, might have proved God's noblest friends and humanity's strongest helpers!

By the exigency of war and the interposition of Jehovah, slavery in America was brought to an end in 1865. One year later young Walker's mother died. From this time on young Charles was left to his own resources. Moving about as best he could from one relative to another, finally, in 1873, he went to work as a farm hand for his uncle, the Rev. Nathan Walker. This uncle had by this time come to be a large planter in his own right, and was renting hundreds of acres of land from his former masters.

Wednesday before the first Sunday in June, 1873, while young Walker was hoeing cotton, he decided to seek the Lord. When he reached the end of the row, without saying a word to anybody, he jumped over the fence and went into the woods. Without eating or drinking, and without seeing any one, he remained in the woods until the following Saturday afternoon, when he was happily converted. He had remained in the woods three days and three nights. How like the blessed Chri t, who laid in the grave three days and three nights and then rose triumphant over death, hell and the grave! This strange way of seeking the Lord, this strange conversion, as it might be called, was all the more remarkable when it is understood that there was no great wave of religious revival sweeping over Richmond County. A short time before this there had been special prayer services in which there had been numbers of conversions; but young Walker's conversion was the result of quiet and serious meditation on his own part and an earnest desire to be a meek and lowly follower of the Lamb.

Young Walker joined the Franklin Covenant Baptist Church, near Hephzibah, and was baptized into the fellowship of that church the first Sunday in July, 1873. The ceremony was performed by his uncle, the Rev. Nathan Walker, the pastor of the church and the man by whom he was at that time employed. This was the same church of which another uncle, the Rev. Joseph T. Walker, had been pastor during the days of slavery, and of which young Walker's father was once a deacon. At the time of his baptism, young Walker was fifteen years old.

CHAPTER III.

THE STUDENT PERIOD.

From the time of his conversion, young Walker was an active and zealous Christian, and at once became prominently identified with every branch of church work—the prayer meeting, the Sunday school and the preaching service. He had not been long converted before he was deeply impressed with the thought that he was called of God to preach the gospel. He felt, nevertheless, that he must restrain this desire until he had acquired some education. He had been taught his A, B, C's by his mother. She had also taught him to read the fourteenth chapter of John. He has preserved to this day the old Bible from which his mother taught him to read. It is needless to say that his mother's Bible is to him a priceless treasure. Subsequently his entire schooling had been confined to two terms of five months each in the schools conducted in Augusta, Ga., by the Freedman's Bureau. His first teachers were two Northern young ladies, Miss Hattie Dow and Miss Hattie Foote. In order to secure better school advantages, and in order to fit himself for his life work, he came to Augusta in 1874 and entered the Augusta Institute, a school which was specially designed for colored preachers. This school was presided over by the late Rev. Joseph T. Robert, LL. D. Dr. Robert was a native of South Carolina and had been a slaveholder.

After emancipation, he felt moved of God to take up the work of training Negro young men for the Christian ministry. He wrought well in his day and generation; he made the Augusta Institute a great school; no man, before or since his time, has left a deeper impress upon the history of the Negro Baptists of Georgia; and there is no man whose name is more honored and revered among them. He was a polished and scholarly gentleman of the old school; he possessed a great degree of what is called personal magnetism; and, by his upright living and Christian fervor, he had the power of inspiring his pupils to higher and nobler things. In the autumn of 1879, Augusta Institute was moved to Atlanta, and the name was changed to Atlanta Baptist Seminary. More recently the name has been changed to Atlanta Baptist College. It is still the largest and most influential school for young men in Georgia, and is regarded as the headquarters of the Negro Baptist ministers in the State.

In school young Walker was soon celebrated for his thoroughness, his exemplary deportment, and for his native talent. He had only six dollars in money when he entered school. With this he rented a room in a private family, for which he paid two dollars per month. In this room he lived during his first year in the Augusta Institute. He did his own washing and cooking—cooking only twice a week, on Wednesdays and Saturdays. He did this in order to save time for study and to keep down expenses. He had only one suit of clothes, which he used on Sundays as well as on week days. When he had exhausted his six dollars, he picked up his little bundle, and was on the verge of leaving school, having decided to walk back to the country and find work to enable him to re-enter school at the opening of the next school year. Some of his friends among the students, finding out the reason for his proposed departure, remonstrated with him and, presenting him a small sum of money, urged him to be patient a day or two longer. One of his fellow students, the late Rev. E. K. Love, D. D., of Savannah, Ga., went so far as to agree to provide for Mr. Walker until other arrangements could be made. In the course of time this same Dr. Love came to be, all things considered, one of the brainiest and most brilliant Negro preachers in America, and as an organizer of men in religion, education, politics or business, he was probably unequaled by any of his contemporaries. For fourteen years he pastored the largest Negro church in the world—the First African Baptist Church, Savannah, Ga. At the time of his death in 1900, Dr. Walker, who came all the way from New York to Georgia to speak at his funeral, referred with much feeling and tenderness to the strong ties of personal friendship which had so closely bound them for years, and spoke with gratitude of Dr. Love's ready assistance to him during his student days.

Through some of the students, Dr. Robert, the President of the Augusta Institute, was informed of young Walker's sad plight, and, through Dr. Robert, three gentlemen in Dayton, Ohio—Mr. G. N. Bierce, Mr. A. B. Solomon, and Mr. E. B. Crawford—became interested in him, and, through the kindness of these three men, he was enabled to prosecute his studies at the Augusta Institute for five years. Two of these three gentlemen—Mr. Bierce and Mr. Solomon—are still living. Both are still very wealthy, and are among Ohio's most successful business men. In November, 1901, Mr. Bierce went to New York to attend the Jubilee Dinner of the International Y. M. C. A. While in New York, he visited Dr. Walker at his home, went with him to the church which he serves as pastor, and also to the Colored Branch of the Y. M. C. A., 132 W. 53rd St., which was founded by Dr. Walker. In his speech at the Colored Men's Branch, Mr. Bierce, among other things, said that he had made many investments in his life, but he believed that the money he had invested in Dr. Walker's education had yielded the largest and best returns of any investment that he had ever made. He also told how he came to be interested in the elevation of the colored race. He said that during the late Civil War he was a soldier in the Union Army, and had drifted with his regiment into Kentucky. While there he was seriously wounded and left for dead on the battlefield. After many hours he managed to make his way to the house of a white Southerner, and asked for shelter and food. Seeing that Mr. Bierce was a Union soldier, the white Southerner denied him both, but called one of his colored servants and told him that he might take charge of the man and care for him, if he desired to do so. The colored man took charge of Mr. Bierce, and, in their lonely cabin, the colored man and his wife carefully watched and nursed the wounded soldier, and in a few weeks brought him back to health and strength. After the war, Mr. Bierce made many efforts to find these faithful Good Samaritans and reward them for their kindness. Failing in this, he decided that, as he owed his life to the attention and care of two members of the Negro race, he would let no opportunity pass to help any of the race who might need assistance. And true to his pledge, Mr. Bierce has been the steady and consistent friend of the colored people from that day to this. Dr. Walker is only one of many beneficiaries of his kindness, and Dr. Walker is a conspicuous example of what a little money, wisely placed in the education of one colored man, can do toward the elevation of an entire race.

Though Dr. Walker finished the prescribed course at the Augusta Institute, he was not graduated from that institution. No graduates were sent out from that school until long after it had been moved to Atlanta, the first class being regularly graduated in 1884. Subsequently, by vote of the trustees, it was decided that the names of nearly fifty young men who had finished the prescribed course prior to 1884, should be placed in the catalogue and marked "entitled to rank as graduates." Dr. Walker's name is in this number. But whether graduated or not, Dr. Walker easily excels any man who was graduated there, and no man, living or dead, has ever heard him express any regret that he does not hold a diploma.

In September, 1876, after two years in the Augusta Institute, and in the eighteenth year of his age, young Walker was licensed to preach. The first Sunday in May, 1877, he was ordained to the sacred office of the Gospel ministry.

HOME OF PETER WALKER, NEAR HEPHZIBAH, GA., WHERE CHARLES T. WALKER LIVED DURING THE FIRST EIGHT YEARS OF HIS LIFE.

CHAPTER IV.

EARLY PASTORATES.

The Rev. Mr. Walker soon became noted as a preacher in and around Augusta. Possessing a fair knowledge of the Bible, and at all times an earnest and enthusiastic speaker, the people literally crowded to hear the "boy preacher," as the Rev. C. T. Walker, on account of his age and youthful appearance, was called for a good many years after he entered the ministry. October 1st, 1877, he was called to the pastorate of the Franklin Covenant Baptist Church, near Hephzibah, and assumed the duties of the office on the first day of January, 1878. This was the church of which he was a member, of which his father had been a deacon, and of which, before him, two of his uncles had been pastors. Calls to other churches followed in rapid succession, and by the time he reached his twenty-first birthday, February, 1879, he was pastor of the four following churches: Franklin Covenant Baptist Church, near Hephzibah, Ga.; Thankful Baptist Church, Waynesboro, Ga.; McKinnie's Branch Baptist Church, Burke County, Ga., and Mount Olive Baptist Church, in the suburbs of of Augusta, Ga. If it seem strange that one man should be the pastor of so many churches, it may be stated that it is customary in the country districts of the South for one preacher to be in charge of several churches. He will give about one Sunday in every month to each church. Sometimes the churches served by one pastor are all in the same county. Sometimes they are separated by many miles. Of course, no real pastoral work can be done in this way. Of necessity the people suffer; no continuous, well-organized spiritual training can be kept up. But, as a rule, the country churches are unable to properly pay their pastors, and but for this system which allows one minister to pastor several churches, there are many churches which would be without any pastor. Even under the present system it is very difficult for the majority of pastors to secure anything like proper remuneration.

The Rev. Mr. Walker, nevertheless, was not to be doomed to the drudgery of pastoring several churches at one and the same time. After a little more than one year's service, he resigned all of his other churches to become pastor of the First Baptist Church at LaGrange, Ga., in the early part of 1880.

It was with very great regret that the churches which he had been serving consented to his withdrawal. Two of them voted to increase his salary if he would decide to continue to serve them. He had done good service, and these struggling churches felt that it would be difficult to find any one who would be able to serve as well, as faithfully, and as acceptably as he had done. Hence, they objected to his removal. Especially was it hard for him to withstand the entreaties of his home church. The members of the Franklin Covenant Baptist Church held a mass meeting protesting against the withdrawal of their pastor and urging him to remain with his own people. When he announced to them his final decision, to the effect that he felt that the Lord was calling him to the new field of labor and that he would obey what he believed to be the call of the Holy Spirit, the whole congregation broke down in tears. It was a sad and trying experience in the life of the young preacher.

During the summer months of 1876, 1877, 1878 and 1879, the Rev. Mr. Walker taught school in the Franklin Covenant Baptist Church building. That is another thing that is peculiar to the rural districts of the South. In many places, perhaps in the majority of places, the public schools are conducted in church edifices, the States having no funds for buildings for schools and the people, as a rule, the white people as well as the colored people, being too poor to erect separate school buildings, find it convenient to use the church building for school purposes. As a school-teacher he was successful, so far as the conditions of the time and his own attainments warranted. It must be confessed, none the less, that he taught school as a means of support and to help him in paying his own expenses while attending the Augusta Institute.

June 19th, 1879, Rev. Mr. Walker was married to Miss Violet O. Franklin, of Hephzibah, Ga. To them four children were born. Three children are dead. One son is still living—Master Jonathan Walker, a lad yet in his teens. One daughter, Mrs. Alberta Walker Hughes, left a daughter at her death, and this grandchild is pet of Dr. Walker and wife.

Dr. Walker remained in LaGrange for nearly three years. While there he was a busy, active, energetic, influential and successful pastor. It was while there that he gave promise of his future eminence as a soul-stirring, soul-saving evangelist. He conducted two of the most eventful revivals ever held in Western Georgia. More than four hundred souls were savingly converted, and more than three hundred were added to the church which he pastored. After these meetings, he received many invitations to conduct series of meetings in the leading Georgia cities, and accepted as many as he could well afford to accept without injury to his own work at LaGrange. At LaGrange he also established a school for Baptists, and was instrumental in having a large frame building erected for this purpose. The school finally grew into the La Grange Academy, a large and influential Baptist High School. It was at LaGrange, also, that he read law for nearly two years under Judge Walker, one of the ablest members of the Georgia bar, and, though he was never admitted to the bar, it is evident that his legal learning has stood him in good stead in the exposition of many a Scripture passage, and, though the law may have lost a brilliant expounder, it is certain that a great leader and teacher was saved to the church and religion.

CHAPTER V.

THE WORK AT AUGUSTA.

The Rev. Charles T. Walker was called to the pastorate of the Central Baptist Church at Augusta, Ga., in 1883, and resigned the First Baptist Church at LaGrange to enter upon the work at Augusta. Central Baptist Church is one of the oldest churches in Augusta, and was the first colored church in the city to erect a brick building. The edifice was very large and was a credit to the city. But for nearly twelve months before the Rev. Mr. Walker was elected pastor, the church had been engaged in a very unfortunate wrangle. The Rev. Henry Jackson was the predecessor of Rev. Walker, and he had been the pastor of the church almost from its organization in 1858. A daughter of Rev. Jackson was the organist of the church, and it seems that the pastor wanted her salary increased. The majority of the deacons and trustees did not agree with the pastor; but the pastor called a business meeting of the church, and, by high-handed methods, so it was claimed, succeeded in having a vote passed favoring the proposed increase in the organist's pay. From that day the wrangle started in good earnest. There were charges and counter-charges. There were plots and counter-plots. The faction favoring the pastor was called "Jacksonites," and the opposing faction was called "Ramrackers." The deacons were divided; the trustees were divided; the membership was divided. There was scarcely a meeting held at the church for any purpose but that there were harsh words passed on both sides, and sometimes there were fisticuffs. Many

FRANKLIN COVENANT BAPTIST CHURCH.

THE FIRST CHURCH PASTORED BY REV. C. T. WALKER. THE PRESENT EDIFICE WAS ERECTED UNDER HIS ADMINISTRATION.

police trials resulted from these disgraceful occurrences. Once the lights were put out during a meeting. In the darkness, some miscreant sent a pistol ball crashing through one of the windows. Pandemonium reigned within. The church was locked up several times by injunctions sued out before the courts—sometimes by one side, sometimes by the other. Finally, the trouble became so acute that it was positively unsafe for any one to attend the church. There came a temporary lull in the warfare of the saints (?) when the Rev. Henry Jackson resigned and left the city. For a time the factions seemed to have settled their differences. The church came together and extended a unanimous call to the Rev. C. T. Walker to take up the pastorate. After much deliberation and prayer, the Rev. Mr. Walker accepted the call. He was twenty-five years old at the time, but looked to be much younger. From the beginning he made a favorable impression. His first sermon was preached the fourth Sunday in August, 1883, from these words: "For I am determined not to know anything among you, save Jesus Christ, and him crucified" (1 Cor. 2:2). Those who were present on the occasion of this introductory sermon remember vividly the preacher's sermon and his appearance. A youngish looking man of medium height and rather slim, with frank, open features; face very dark; quiet of demeanor and graceful in movement; with a sweet, clear, orotund voice, enunciating every word distinctly. With the man and the sermon, the church and congregation were alike delighted and encouraged; and never did they seem to sing before with such thrilling effect and such depths of meaning, "Blest be the tie that binds."

But church wars never end. Whatever may have been the outward appearances, those on the inside knew that, though all said that they had buried the hatchet, some of them at least had left the hatchet's handle sticking a good way out of the ground. None knew this better than the new young pastor, and none grieved more because of it. "The Jacksonites" wanted to direct the policy of the new minister, and so did the "Ramrackers." Each side was jealous of the other, and, although siding with neither, the new pastor found himself at every stem of his journey between two fires. Consequently, though earnestly desiring to do the Lord's work and praying daily to learn God's will, he was an unhappy man. The troubles continued. By and by the church reached the point where it felt that to discipline a few of the recalcitrant officers might help matters some. The action of the church not suiting the "Jacksonites," the church was again closed by injunction, and the whole affair was dragged again into the courts. By the advice of lawyers on both sides, since it seemed impossible to harmonize the differences, it was agreed that the church should be sold and the proceeds equally divided between the representatives of the two factions. Accordingly, the church was sold at pubilc outcry. It was bid in by the "Jacksonites." The "Ramrackers," so-called, received something over $2,000 for the sale. The "Jacksonites" took charge of the old church, reorganized and called the Rev. Henry Jackson as pastor. The other side, under the leadership of the Rev. Mr. Walker, worshipped temporarily in the hall of the Union Waiters' Society on Ellis Street, the hall being generously donated by the Society for that purpose. Friday night, August 21st, 1885, this body was formally organized at the Union Baptist Church, under the name of Beulah Baptist Church. The enrolled membership at the time of organization was 310—115 males and 195 females. At a special business meeting at the close of the service Sunday night, August 23, 1885, at the suggestion of the pastor, the name of the church was changed from Beulah Baptist Church to Tabernacle Baptist Church. Plans were at once set on foot for the erection of a house of worship. Proper committees were appointed. A lot was secured on Ellis Street, above 10th Street, and work was commenced on the new building September 1st, 1885. September 10th, the corner stone was laid with appropriate ceremonies, the address being delivered by the late Rev. E. K. Love, D. D., of Savannah, Ga. The building was opened for worship and formally dedicated to the Lord the second Sunday in December, being the 13th day, 1885. The dedicatory sermon was preached at the morning service by the Rev. E. R. Carter, D. D., of Atlanta, Ga., from this text: "But will God indeed dwell on the earth? Behold the heaven and heaven of heavens cannot contain thee; how much less this house that I have builded?" (1 King 8:27.) The afternoon sermon was delivered by the Rev. Lansing Burrows, D. D., the well known Secretary of the Southern (white) Baptist Convention and for a long time editor of the American Baptist Year Book. The sermon at night was delivered by the late Rev. Dr. E. K. Love.

The Tabernacle Baptist Church edifice is built of brick, two stories high. The basement is used for the prayer meetings, the Sunday School, the pastor's study, and closets. The auditorium upstairs is used for the preaching services and for lectures. It will seat comfortably about 800 persons. It cost (for ground and building) $13,500. Dedicated within three months after it was commenced and paid for within less than two years after it was completed, including a new pipe organ costing $1,500, is a record which has probably not been surpassed by any colored congregation in the South, and speaks well for the ability and zeal of the leader. With a new church building and with a sterling and brilliant young pastor, Tabernacle Baptist Church soon became the leading colored church in Augusta, a city noted for its splendid churches and its able pastors. It was while he was with this church that the Rev. C. T. Walker made his reputation as a pulpit orator, a sound theologian, a soul-winning evangelist, and a resourceful pastor. At the close of fourteen years of hard labor, Oct. 1st, 1899, it was found from the records of the church clerk that more than 2,000 souls had been converted during his ministry, and that more than 1,400 had been baptized by him into the fellowship of the Tabernacle Baptist Church.

It was in connection with the work at Tabernacle Church that the pastor made his first extended tour throughout New York and New England. The members of the church had by their own efforts paid nearly $10,000 of the $13,500, which was the total cost of their ground and building. In the autumn of 1886, the pastor, armed with numerous testimonials and letters of introduction, went North to solicit funds to assist in completing the payments on the church property. He found ready acceptance and willing ears everywhere he went. It was at this time that he preached for the first time in Mt. Olivet Baptist Church, 161 W. 53rd Street, New York city, of which years afterwards he became pastor. Of his visit to the Centennial Baptist Church, Brooklyn, the pastor, the late Rev. Dr. Justin Dewey Fulton, wrote: "My people who heard him pronounce him a preacher of more than ordinary ability. His voice is good, his bearing modest and impressive, his language excellent, and the aim of his preaching is to glorify Christ." In other churches and in other cities, the Rev. Mr.

Walker found similar warm friends, who listened eagerly to his exposition of God's word or to his appeals for aid in his work at the South. He returned to his work in Georgia, satisfied with the financial results of his trip, but more gratified with the moral support and encouragement he received. In reporting his labors to his members on his return, the Rev. Mr. Walker said, among other things: "The Lord went with me, and opened up for me many places which were considered very hard, and enabled me to approach some persons who were at first apparently not at all friendly toward the colored people. When I got on the grounds and learned the true situation, I was not at all disposed to criticise the people of the North for being cautious about distributing their money to irresponsible persons. I found out that numbers of colored people go up North every year begging for money for churches and schools and orphan homes and the like, which have no existence at all, except in the imaginations of their impostors or on paper. When members of my own race will do such things they make it hard for a worthy person soliciting for a worthy and legitimate enterprise and you cannot blame people for being careful about giving their money when they know that there are many little schemes being worked by colored men to rob them. 'A burnt child dreads the fire,' and the good have to suffer on account of the conduct of those who are dishonest and speculative. But God was with me and directed me, and I secured a hearing and received contributions in some places where others were denied. We should all be thankful for this, as much as any thing else. It pays to be honest, sincere and straightforward, and I have no patience with those hypocrites who are systematically robbing the good people of the North, who are very willing to give of their means for the uplift of my downtrodden race."

REV. CHARLES T. WALKER AT TWENTY-FIVE YEARS OF AGE.

CHAPTER VI.

OTHER WORK AT AUGUSTA.

Not only was the Rev. Mr. Walker notably successful as a pastor while he lived in Augusta, but he was also a very active citizen, taking a prominent part in all enterprises looking to the betterment of the people along educational, religious and business lines. It may be said with truth that his public spirit, his generous concern for the welfare of all the people, was one of the things that gave point and power to his preaching and caused "the common people" to hear him gladly.

In 1884, the Augusta Sentinel, a weekly paper, was established by Prof. R. R. Wright, A. M. (afterwards Major R. R. Wright, LL. D.), who was at that time Principal of the Ware High School. The Rev. Mr. Walker was one of its largest stockholders and was elected Business Manager. In 1891, Prof. Wright left the editorship of the paper to become the first President of the Georgia State Industrial College, near Savannah, Ga., a position which he still holds. Major Wright was and is one of Georgia's leading educators and most representative citizens. He has represented his State four or five times in Republican National Conventions, and was appointed a "Major and Additional Paymaster" in the U. S. V. by the late President McKinley during the Spanish-American war. When Prof. Wright left the editorial chair, he was succeeded by the late Rev. E. K. Love, D. D., of Savannah, Ga. Dr. Love retired in 1892, and was succeeded by Prof. Silas X. Floyd.

But, through all these changes, the Rev. Dr. Walker remained in charge of the business department of the paper until it died a natural death in 1896. In 1891, while Dr. Walker was traveling in Europe and the Holy Land, he sent a weekly letter to the Sentinel, and these letters did much in adding to the popularity of the paper. On his return, these letters were compiled and published in a volume of 148 pp. 16 mo. under the name and title of "A Colored Man Abroad." The book had a wide sale and found many readers.

The Walker Baptist Association in 1880 passed a resolution to establish a high and normal school for colored children. Dr. Walker was the author of that resolution. The school was at first located at Waynesboro, Ga., where it remained for about three years. Dr. Walker became convinced that the school would thrive better if it was moved to Augusta, and he was specially anxious to have the school removed to that place, because he desired to see a good school conducted by Baptists in Augusta, a city of Baptists, and in which the Methodists and Presbyterians were already conducting creditable normal schools. It was mainly through Dr. Walker's efforts that the school was finally moved to Augusta in 1891, and even the most doubtful have been led by subsequent events to appreciate the wisdom of his suggestion. The school is now a large and flourishing institution, occupying a commanding site, the chapel, class rooms, dormitory and grounds being valued at something over $5,000. The school is unemcumbered, owned and controlled by the colored Baptists, assisted to a very limited extent by the American Baptist Home Mission Society. From the beginning, Dr. Walker has been the Financial Agent of the school, which position he still holds. He has succeeded in bringing to its support a large number of friends, both white and black, North and South. It is one of his fond dreams for the future to establish in connection with this school a large Industrial School and Business College. His friends believe that it will not be difficult for him to accomplish this, because the work already done by the colored people themselves in connection with this school, the excellent showing they have made in the direction of self-help, will commend itself to a generous public wherever it is told.

In 1893, the colored people of Augusta organized an exposition company. This company held an exposition that year, commencing December 18 and running through one week. The officers of the company were Bishop R. S. Williams, of the C. M. E. Church, President; Prof. Silas X. Floyd, Editor Augusta Sentinel, Secretary; Mr. Charles J. Floyd, Assistant Secretary; Mr. George J. Scott, a grocer, Treasurer, and Dr. C. T. Walker, Director-General. Exhibits were on hand from colored undertakers, colored cabinet makers, colored harness makers, shoemakers, contractors, carpenters and brick masons, printers, wheelwrights, carriage and wagon makers, farmers, who exhibited farm products, cattle, swine, poultry and the like, dressmakers, needle and fancy work by colored girls and young women, colored artists, who exhibited oil paintings, lanscape paintings and sketches in charcoal and crayon, colored bakers, tailors, electricians, school-teachers, and the like. In his address to the public, Director-General Walker said: "Primarily, the basic principle upon which the Negro Exposition is founded is a desire to show to the world the advancement and progress made by the American Negro, especially the Southern Negro, and most especially the Georgia Negro, within the past thirty years. But no such exposition can be held in Augusta

THE WALKER BAPTIST INSTITUTE, AUGUSTA, GA., FOUNDED BY DR. CHARLES T. WALKER.

without also resulting in a general advantage to the interests of the city." Evidently, the city council of Augusta, composed entirely of white Southern men, took the view held by the Director-General, for, upon request for aid from the Directors of the Negro Exposition Company, the city council appropriated $200 from the city treasury for the promotion of the enterprise, and gave six policeman and all fire protection free. The exposition was a creditable display of the Negro's progress, and did much to illustrate the purposes for which it was organized. The Director-General was present every day and had charge of the program. The welcome address was delivered by the mayor of the city, Major J. H. Alexander, to nearly 5,000 colored people and many hundreds of white people on the opening day, Monday, December 18, 1893. At the conclusion of the address of welcome, the formal opening address was delivered by the Rev. E. R. Carter, D. D., of Atlanta, Ga., one of the most popular Southern Negro orators. Tuesday, December 19, was Educational Day. All the public and private schools of the city had a general holiday in honor of the event. More than 2,000 school children marched early in the morning of that day behind brass bands to the Exposition Grounds, where appropriate exercises were held. Speeches were delivered by Prof. Lawton B. Evans, Superintendent of Schools, Augusta, Ga., and Prof. R. R. Wright, A. M. Music was furnished by a trained choir of 500 voices of public school children under the direction of Prof. A. R. Johnson. Wednesday, December 20, was Military Day. The address of the day was delivered by Congressman George W. Murray, of South Carolina, after which there was a spirited prize drill by the various companies. Thursday, December 21, was Firemen's Day. A mammoth street parade of twelve fire companies took place in the forenoon, and, in the afternoon, there were reel races, foot races, bicycle races, and a base ball game. Friday was Vaudeville Day. Mason and Johnson's Ethiopian Minstrels gave performances afternoon and evening. Saturday afternoon the exhibition closed with a grand industrial parade on the Exposition Grounds. The like had never been seen before in this country, and probably has not been seen since. To no one was more credit due for the success of the entire affair than to the indefatigable Director-General, the Rev. Dr. Walker. He gave himself to the work both night and day without receiving one cent of pay.

In these public ways and in others, Dr. Walker made his presence in Augusta known and felt. But not alone for his public spirit is he known, honored and loved by the people of Augusta, as is no other man who has labored there, but also for the rendering of many private acts of sympathy and help and encouragement, which the world does not know about, and which the world cannot know about. The number of those whom he has been instrumental in saving from the jails, chain gangs and penitentiary; those he has had released from imprisonment, whose fines he has paid out of his own pocket; the number whose house rent he has paid, and furnished food, and clothing, and fuel; the number of unhappy husbands he has reconciled to unhappy wives, thereby making both happy again; the young people he has sent to school and has helped to educate; the men and women for whom he has secured employment; those he has brought to Christ by private ministrations; the number he has encouraged and cheered by a kind act or a "word fitly spoken;" the number he has helped and inspired in one way and another, will reach far into the thousands. The number cannot be known

"Until the sun grows cold,
And the stars are old,
And the leaves of the Judgment Book unfold."

Dr. Walker did these things as if by second nature, and, though now and then friends remonstrated with him and told him that he ought not to allow others to impose upon him, he went straight ahead, quietly and unostentatiously, spending and being spent for the Master, and his heart filled with the milk of human kindness, he lent a listening ear and an outstretched arm to every cry for pity and every appeal for help.

THE TABERNACLE OLD FOLKS' HOME, AUGUSTA, GA., FOUNDED BY DR. CHARLES T. WALKER.

CHAPTER VII.

INFLUENCE IN GEORGIA.

In spite of his arduous labors and duties at Augusta, Dr. Walker yet found time to be interested in all matters which concerned the welfare of all the people throughout the State of Georgia, and was an active participant in many State gatherings of various kinds, aside from the large number of evangelistic meetings he found time to conduct in many Georgia cities. For several years he was Moderator of the Western Union Baptist Association; for four or five years he was Chairman of the Executive Board of the Missionary Baptist Convention of Georgia; for two years he was Vice President, and for eight years Secretary of the same body; he was Treasurer for several years of the Sunday School Workers' Convention of Georgia; he was at one time Vice President of the Georgia Interdenominational Sunday School Convention; he was for a number of years a member of the Republican State Executive Committee; he has been, from the beginning, a member of the Board of Trustees of the Walker Baptist Institute, and was also a member of the Board of Trustees of the Atlanta Baptist College. The filling of these various offices of trust and responsibility indicate in a small way the immense activity which he has displayed in the general welfare of the State, and particularly the welfare of the Baptist denomination.

In addition to these things, there has not been a convention of any kind called by the colored citizens of Georgia, as has frequently been the case during the past twenty years, which he has not attended, anxious always to do something to advance the Negro in the scale of civilization. He has many times visited the annual meetings of the State Teachers' Association of Georgia and, by invitation, has adressed them, trying to show what part the teachers ought to take in solving the so-called "Race Problem." He has been a favorite commencement orator at many of Georgia's schools and colleges, and has never been able in any one year to accept all the numerous invitations which have come to him to deliver baccalaureate sermons. On the first day of January each year, it is customary for the colored people throughout the South to hold public meetings, where addresses are delivered by distinguished men, in commemoration of the issuing of the Emancipation Proclamation by Abraham Lincoln, Jan. 1st, 1863. Dr. Walker's addresses, delivered at different places in the State on Emancipation Day, would alone make a very large and interesting volume. Nor has he felt that his duties as a preacher have of necessity absolved him from active participation in public affairs, or what is more generally called politics. He was for years a member of the Richmond County Executive Committee of the Republican Party, and also a member of the Republican State Committee. He has believed and has taught that it is the duty of every citizen to be interested in the political welfare of his city, State and country, and, in his judgment, no man is entitled to be called a good citizen who allows the vicious and corrupt to do all the voting and all the dictating, and then sits down and sighs for what is called "the better and purer days of the Republic." Of his work as an evangelist, mention will be made in a later chapter. But let it be said now that no one man in Georgia has held a larger number of special meetings throughout the State, nor has had a larger number of conversions to be attributed to his preaching, than has Dr. Walker. It is not exaggeration to say that he is the best known Negro minister of the State of Georgia, and that more people will go to hear him preach than will go to hear any other colored man. Not the celebrated, plain-spoken, claw and hammer preaching of Sam Jones, nor the Holy Ghost preaching of the pious Dwight L. Moody, of sainted memory, drew larger crowds to the auditorium at Exposition Park, Atlanta, Ga., than did the thunderous proclamation of the gospel by Charles T. Walker.

Perhaps in no way has his influence been felt in Georgia more than in the selection of competent men for Baptist pastorates and in the appointment of competent men and women as teachers at many places in the State. Dr. Walker's reputation as a safe leader and wise counseller, his extensive travels and consequent wide acquaintance with men and women throughout the State and nation have proved to be very helpful to all concerned in the recommendations he has been asked to make. No one in Georgia who knows of these things can recall a single instance in which the recommendation of Dr. Walker, in the case of a church or school, has been turned down. So interested has Dr. Walker been in the welfare of others, and so eager has he been to see competent leaders set over the people, that he has been known time and again to go 500, 600, and sometimes 1,000 miles at his own expense to assist those who needed and asked his opinion and advice, or to help some person to secure a position. Not all of those whom he has helped have been grateful; not all of them will admit their obligation; only a few of them remember the bridge that carried them over. When told of the ungratefulness of different ones, Dr. Walker only laughs and says: "I do not help anybody with the expectation of being thanked. It is my duty to do my duty toward my fellow men, whether they thank me or not." Thus he dismisses the subject, and goes to talking about something else. Several times larger churches in Georgia, that could pay him more money than Tabernacle Baptist Church, extended calls to him to occupy their pulpits, but he always replied that Tabernacle Church was good enough for him, and then would assist the churches in securing good men. Such unselfishness is rare, and has helped very much to perpetuate the hold which Dr. Walker has had on the people of Georgia for so many years.

CHAPTER VIII.

THE VISIT TO THE HOLY LAND.

Tabernacle Baptist Church, Augusta, Ga., was the first colored church in this country to send its pastor on a trip to Europe and the Holy Land. This it did in the Spring of 1891. The church voted Dr. Walker a vacation of three months, with full pay, and the church and friends in Augusta, white and colored, furnished money with which to enable him to take the memorable journey. His church was supplied during his absence by the Rev. L. B. Goodall, at that time of Augusta, Ga., now of Charlottesville, Va.

He left Augusta Thursday afternoon, April 9th, 1891, and sailed from New York City on Wednesday, April 15th, at 11 o'clock, a. m., on the steamship *City of New York*, bound for Liverpool. He was accompanied as far as London by the Rev. E. R. Carter, D. D., of Atlanta, Ga., and Prof. M. J. Maddox, at that time, of Gainesville, Fla., now of Savannah, Ga. He visited Liverpool, London, Paris, Turin, Genoa, Pisa, Rome, Pompeii, Alexandria, Cairo, Ismaila, Port Said, Joppa, Jerusalem, Bethlehem, Hebron, Jericho, Bethany, Mount of Olives, Gethsemane, Calvary, Beirut, Cyprus, Smyrna, Ephesus, Pierus, Athens, Corinth, Venice, Patras, Corfu, Brindisi, Basle, Hiedelberg, Mayence, Cologne, Coblenz, Brussels, Antwerp, and some few other places. Dr. Carter accompanied him during the entire journey. He returned to New York on Saturday, June 27th, 1891, and reached Augusta on the fourth day of July.

Before leaving New York on his way to the Holy Land, he preached twice on the Sabbath at the Mt. Olivet Baptist Church, and, at the request of the pastor and officers, he preached again on Monday night, April 13th. The church gave him a liberal contribution to help him on his way, and he departed with their best wishes and with many prayers for a safe journey and a safe return.

The following account taken from the Augusta Evening News, of July 6th, 1891, will give some idea of Dr. Walker's reception on his return to Augusta:

"BETHEL"

"The impressions of an intelligent, zealous and popular colored minister about the Holy Land are well worth hearing and recording.

"The Evening News has already announced the return of the Rev. Chas. T. Walker from his three months' trip abroad, and, indeed, has kept up with him pretty well in his great journey in

FORD OF THE RIVER JORDAN.

Europe, Asia and Africa. The paper was glad to commend him on his departure, and welcomed his return, and these courtesies are both deserved and appreciated. A man who is so highly regarded by his congregation and friends that he is given such a trip, and whose influence is all for good among his people in this community, certainly deserves consideration and courtesy. Hence, more space than ordinary is given to this prominent and popular leader among his people.

"A genuine and hearty welcome was given Mr. Walker by his congregation, and yesterday he preached to his church for the first time in three months. Last night he gave an outline of his trip through the Holy Land, and promised half hour talks about places, scenes and customs for every Sunday evening.

"After reading of the Queen of Sheba's visit to Solomon, he took his text from the famous words, 'the half has not been told,' and declared that those words expressed his ideas about the Holy Land. He did not go into details about his journey, but with a wonderful power of seizing upon leading scenes and incidents and putting them before his audience, with their vivid illustrations and comforting lessons, the preacher held his

SHEEPFOLD.

vast congregation spellbound for about an hour. It was in itself a scene well worth witnessing, to behold this earnest and really eloquent man, with his deep and resonant voice, and genuinely magnetic manner, telling his story to breathless and sympathetic listeners, who crowded every inch of sitting and standing room in the church. This ovation was a great compliment to the humble man of God, who spoke in grateful terms of those who had sent him on his memorable journey; and every one of his people must have felt fully repaid when, in summing up the results of his trip and the analysis of his observations, he declared that, after seeing and investigating the Holy Land for himself, he

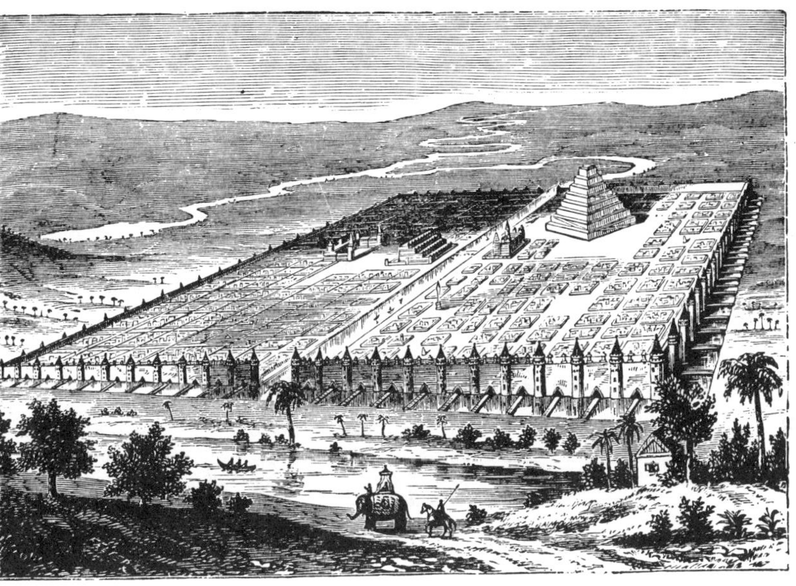

BABYLON.

felt more than ever that God's word was true. If any one is sceptical about the Bible, its history and its sacred truths and traditions, said this preacher, let him go to Palestine, and he will be sceptical no longer.

"He also went to Egypt, which is scriptural land, where Moses, the greatest law-maker of the earth, was born, and where Joseph and Abraham, and even Jesus went, and he followed their footsteps back into Palestine, through Joppa, the gateway to Jerusalem, as it also became, through Peter's vision, the doorway of the Gentiles to God's kingdom. The preacher then described the great astronomical miracle performed by Joshua on the plain of Ajalon, when he commanded the sun and moon to stand still;

THE POOL OF SILOAM.

he made graphic references to his journey along the famous highway over which the Roman Emperors and the Christian Crusaders traveled to the Holy City.. Jerusalem, with its four mountains, its old walls, its eight gates, its well-remembered streets, was particularly dwelt upon, and the speaker declared that it was hard for him to realize that he was actually in the great city where the prophets walked, which was blessed by the Saviour's presence and consecrated by his crucifixion. He went straight to Calvary, he said, and his description of Calvary, as the greatest battle field the world ever saw, was very interesting, and was one of the most eloquent and vividly touching portions of his discourse. The effect on the

AN EASTERN HARVEST SCENE.

audience was realistic and remarkable. The people leaned forward, and as the preacher alluded to Calvary as the greatest battle-field the world ever saw and said that the cross was its eternal monument, murmurs and shouts of approval went up all over the house.

"The Church of the Holy Sepulchre, the Tomb of the Saviour, Gethsemane, the Brook Kedron, and the Mount of Olives, were in turn dwelt upon; and the minister said that as he bowed and wept at the Saviour's Tomb, he arose refreshed and wrote in his note-book: 'Thank God, he is a resurrected Jesus.'

"In describing the River Jordan, in which he bathed while he was there, and which he visited at the points where Joshua passed over, where Elijah ascended in the chariot, where Naaman was healed, and where Christ was baptized by John, the preacher was again inspired, as he described what he said was the most glorious convocation that ever took place on earth—when the Trinity met at the Saviour's baptism.

"In impressing the truth of the Scriptures, Mr. Walker used several striking illustrations. He said that the old prophecies

BAPTIZING IN THE RIVER JORDAN.

were coming true, and that even the Turks, in their ignorance, were fulfilling prophecy. They keep the Golden Gate—the Gate Beautiful—always closed, the only one entering Jerusalem which is never opened, because the superstitious believe that if the Christians ever enter by it, they will retake the city; but the minister declared that the real reason was that it was a fulfillment of Eze-

ARAB ENCAMPMENT.

kiel's prophecy found in the forty-fourth chapter of his writings. Again, Jeremiah said, twenty-five hundred years ago, that 'Zion shall be ploughed like a field.' The people of a then rich and powerful city came near stoning him for his madness, and yet the speaker declared, with his own eyes he had seen the fulfillment of this prophecy. Jeremiah also declared that Zion should be rebuilt, and on the unearthed ruins of the very towers indicated by Jeremiah, the rebuilding of Jerusalem had been begun. To-day, they are rebuilding, as the prophet said. In Jerusalem and all through Palestine, the record speaks in solemn, sacred and rock-ribbed confirmation of the blessed and everlasting truth of God's word.

"The preacher concluded with a strong invocation, and declared that after all his journeyings over oceans and seas, there was no sailing like sailing with Jesus, and he had come back home with sevenfold more of the spirit of the Saviour to stir up the people of the city with the truth of the Gospel. We all need more power and less form; more of the power of Charles Spurgeon, whose power and influence and magnetism come from communing with God.

"He paid a telling tribute to this country when he said that he would not exchange it for any he had seen. He contrasted the terrors and persecutions of heathen lands with the glorious liberty of America, where Christian churches raised their spires to heaven, and all men may worship God according to the dictates of their own consciences, and under their own vine and fig tree. Where there is no church there is no civilization, and he wanted his people to appreciate their advantages, and aid him by doing their duty to God and their fellow men."

Besides his talks and lectures to the people of Augusta, Dr. Walker spent much time during the summer and winter of 1891 lecturing throughout the United States on "The Holy Land: What I Saw and Heard." Everywhere the lecture and the lecturer were well received and highly spoken of—in New York, in Boston, in Philadelphia, in Indianapolis, in Charleston, S. C., in St. Louis, in Dallas and Galveston, Tex., in Kansas City, and in other places. Dr. Walker's success on the lecture platform was immediate, and, since 1891, he has managed each year to go on a little lecture tour through different parts of America.

CHAPTER IX.

A COLORED MAN ABROAD.

Mention has already been made of the fact that while Dr. Walker was traveling abroad he wrote weekly letters to the Augusta Sentinel, which were compiled on his return and published in book form, under the name and style of "A Colored Man Abroad." Extracts from that publication will serve not only to show Dr. Walker's literary style, but will also be of interest, instruction and entertainment to the reader.

Dr. Walker's letters from the Holy Land were written for the most part from notes taken on the ground, somewhat as one would keep a diary or a sailor's log. The second day out from New York, he paid the following

TRIBUTE TO THE SEA.

"The sea is a revelation of the omnipotence of the Almighty! It carries with perfect ease upon its bosom the greatest ships that circumnavigate the globe. It is the home of numerous animals, small and great, as well as the pathway of Jehovah. It is also the tomb of hundreds of thousands of human beings; for the sea has wrecked hundreds of vessels and sailing craft, and holds entombed the bodies of countless shipwrecked people. As we look at the sea, we are reminded of the grand old words of Byron:

'Roll on, thou deep and dark blue ocean, roll,
Ten thousand fleets sweep over thee in vain;

Man marks the earth with ruin,—his control
Stops with the shore,—upon the watery plain
The wrecks are all thy deed, nor doth remain
A shadow of man's ravage, save his own,
When for a moment, like a drop of rain,
He sinks into thy depth with bubbling groan,
Without a grave, unknelled, uncoffined and unknown.' "

In the following words, Dr. Walker describes his

FIRST SABBATH AT SEA.

"It is Sunday morning. The day is calm, and the sun is shining brightly. Divine services were held in the chapel at 10:30 a. m., conducted by the captain, who read the Episcopal service. A Sabbath at sea is a sad day to those who love the house of God. No church bell is heard calling the people to their respective places of worship. No soul-inspiring anthems are sung. No heartfelt prayers are heard ascending like sweet incense from the altar of praise. We miss the pulpit ministration and the Christian greeting that come from the gentle throbbing of loving and affectionate hearts. We miss the Sunday school, where the little folks are singing their many beautiful songs, expressive of our dear Saviour's life and love. In place of all this, we observe men drinking and carousing and engaged in all kinds of frivolity; we see many women and girls reading novels, but not one perusing the Bible. Give me no more Sabbaths in mid-ocean."

The first Sunday in London, Dr. Walker visited Spurgeon's church. Following is his description of

SPURGEON'S TABERNACLE.

"Spurgeon's Tabernacle is the greatest church on earth, and its pastor is undoubtedly the grandest preacher in the universe. Eternity alone can tell the good this man of God is doing. Seven thousand people hear him twice on each Lord's Day. He has a Baptist College, perfect in its every appointment, a missionary society, a tract society, a place for the poor, an orphan home, a mission station conducted by the young men of his congregation, a printing press, and everything else in the line of an active, live and progressive church. Here the 'rich and the poor meet together; and the Lord is the maker of them all.' The doctrine of the fatherhood of God and the universal brotherhood of man is taught with all the earnestness of which this good man is capable. In this Tabernacle, you will find men and women who are worth thousands and ten thousands of pounds sterling out in the streets and alleys of London, bringing the poor, the wayward, the blasphemer, the halt and the blind to hear Spurgeon preach. We heard him on the Sabbath, occupying a seat near him. What a privilege! Two rows of galleries extend all round the edifice. Just below the pastor's stand, there is a gallery for orphan children from the home and those who manage the home. The people are rushing for seats—thousands are already seated, having been admitted because they held quarterly tickets. At five minutes before eleven o'clock, the signal bell is tapped, announcing to all persons who have not secured seats to get them anywhere they can find them, as the holders of tickets have no claim on seats after the tap of the bell. Mr. Spurgeon comes in, followed by his assistant pastor and deacons who take seats near him. He then opens the service with a short, earnest, eloquent prayer that moves many to tears. No organ is used; the chorister stands near the pastor, and the multitude rises and sings a soul-inspiring hymn. The pastor then reads, with exposition, the Scripture lesson. He announces this morning that he will preach the annual missionary sermon. When he begins preaching, seven thousand pairs of eyes are looking steadfastly upon him. He leads the vast audience step by step as he unfolds to them the word of God. Every hearer's heart burns within him. It is a grand sight. I wept as I looked on such a vast throng of people seated in breathless silence, catching the words as they fell from the mouth of God's prophet."

In the month of May, 1891, Dr. Walker spent five days on the Mediterranean Sea en route to Alexandria. While on this sea, famous for its storms, he encountered a storm which he said must have been similar to the one that Paul wrote about in the 27th chapter of the Acts. Following is Dr. Walker's picture of

A STORM ON THE MEDITERRANEAN SEA.

"The sea had been turbulent all night. The fury of the sea continued until noon to-day, when it reached its climax. For nearly an hour the waves united and lashed the steamer in a fearful manner, as if chastening it for disobeying some sea law. We closely watched the treacherous water during the contest. The ship at first seemed to think itself invincible, and had a perfect right to move in its own chosen route, despite the ocean's objection. It was then that the hottest part of the contest took place. The ocean gave one command, and, at that summons, dashing, foaming, giant waves came from every direction to reinforce those already at the scene of battle. When they had combined their forces, they struck the steamer a few times; she cracked, reeled, bowed, tossed herself to and fro, shook up the passengers, made them sick, and put some to bed. Each time the vessel attempted to move out of her tracks she only lifted herself up and came back in the same place. The man on the bridge turned the wheel, but the steamer shook her head. The wind blew, the tempest raged, the captain came from his room, ascended the bridge, took charge of affairs, called up the sailors, gave orders to turn the wheel and let her drive, but she could not go. The sea continued to assert its rights, and when the crew confessed that they were defeated and at the mercy of the waves, they cast anchor, stood still, and waited on the sea to obtain a permit to move forward. The Mediterranean seemed to recognize that the whole crew were baffled, confused and beseeching mercy; so she called in her waves, sent them back to their several stations, each bearing a spray of snowy whiteness as an emblem of the victory they had won. And now all is serene on the water."

Speaking of the people of Syria and other Eastern countries, Dr. Walker wrote the following about the present

MANNERS AND CUSTOMS OF THE EAST.

"The manners and customs of these people are about the same as in the days of Moses, Abraham, Isaac and Jacob. Men work for years to pay for their wives; lead their flocks as David did; dwell in tents; plow oxen as did Elijah; water their fields; sow grain among thorns and rocks; wear the same kind of costumes with the old-time sandals on their feet; use donkeys and camels as beasts of burden—all as in the days of yore. The majority of the Mohammedans and Arabs have no chairs, tables, knives and forks, with no bedsteads in their houses. They eat with their fingers, stretch out on the floor or ground, sleep by the roadside, just as Jacob did when he had his vision. The Mohammedans believe that a person who goes crazy becomes holy. The Turkish government does not allow its subjects to embrace Christianity. To ask a Mohammedan to change his religion is to endanger one's life."

Following is Dr. Walker's notion of

THE TESTIMONY OF THE MOUNTAINS.

"Having made a study of the mountains in this country, they seem to me to wear an air of dignity at once charming and attractive. Lofty, stately, queenly, they look like silent but impressive heralds, standing as reminiscences of the far away past and as landmarks, preserving and perpetuating the history of notable events. Immovable and unchangeable, like their Creator, they have stood while the mighty have fallen; they have witnessed the enthronement and dethronement of kings; the captivity and extermination of nations, and to-day they are almost the only places in Palestine that the searcher after truth may feel safe in pointing out the identical location of Scriptural occurrences. Too lofty and unchangeable for tradition, they are the true historians of past centuries and for ages to come Sinai, Moriah, Carmel, Ebal, Gerizim, Tabor, Beatitudes, Zion and the Mount of Olives will bear witness to the Scriptures in a manner that will be obvious and convincing to the most sceptical mind. Well may Jehovah liken his church to the mountains. And why should not the snow decorate the mountains; the clouds circle about them; the sun linger and play upon their summits; the moon and the stars gaze smilingly upon them, while the lightnings race and prance up and down like electricity from a galvanic battery? Why not the sea crowd the mountain's base, bathe its feet, and perpetually sing sweet anthems to its praise? 'How beautiful upon the mountains are the feet of them that publisheth peace, that say unto Zion, Thy God reigneth.'

Here is Dr. Walker's idea of how some people are heedlessly

DRIFTING ON LIFE'S OCEAN.

"I have been thinking how humanity is drifting on life's ocean. For seven days on the Atlantic, our steamer never stopped. The passengers ate, slept, walked, talked, got sick, some died—but we sailed on. The ship passed other vessels; it was often cloudy; the winds blew; the rains fell; storms and gales were often encountered; the ship caught on fire—but we sailed on. Men gambled, drank whiskey and champagne, cursed and spent their hours in frivolity—and so they sailed on, apparently little dreaming that they were rapidly sailing to that eternal shore from whence no traveler returns."

In view of the recent sad assassination of President McKinley, how like prophecy and solemn warning will the following words, which were written ten years ago, seem. At last, the American congress, at the dictation of President Roosevelt, is turning its attention to this great question which ten years ago Dr. Walker declared must be given some attention. Following is the extract:

ANARCHY—A WARNING.

"In the first-class saloon, there are seventy-six passengers; in the second, sixty; and in the steerage there are about eight hundred—nearly all emigrants. Some are Jews from Russia, fleeing from persecution; others are Belgians, Swedes, Germans, Italians, Irishmen, Welshmen and Scotchmen, all going to our home of freedom—America. Many of them are very immoral, and utterly oblivious of modesty. As a rule, they are a dirty lot, some actually nauseating; and hundreds of them have not washed either their hands or faces on this voyage, so far. Yet these very people come to America to supercede the Negro, and to boss him! These immigrants have extended to them the rights of citizenship in every particular, and yet these inalienable rights are denied the colored man who has helped to make America what it is. Many of these foreigners are of the very worst element in their own country. They are ignorant, treacherous, uncivilized, and many of them heathen. They have no respect for the Sabbath; they have no respect for the law; they have no regard for Christianity; they are antagonistic to the principles of liberty as laid down in the Declaration of Independence of the United States. Mark this prediction: So sure as we live, America is fast getting a Jumbo on her hands. She is nestling a Vesuvius in her bosom that may remain dormant for a long period; but when the volcanic eruption breaks forth, seventy times seven streams of lava will be shot out at one time, and the main pillars that support and uphold the whole fabric of our American institutions will be undermined, uprooted, and partially, if not wholly destroyed. Chicago and New Orleans should be held in remembrance by our whole people, East, West, North and South. The outrages perpetrated by these villains in those cities were comparable to the firing of the first gun on Fort Sumter. Let the American congress spend some time in legislating against these holy terrors, instead of needlessly discussing schemes to deport the poor unfortunate Negro."

CHAPTER X.

AS A NATIONAL FIGURE.

The first National Baptist Convention of Negro Baptists ever held in the United States convened at the Second Baptist Church, St. Louis, Mo., August 25, 1886, at 10 a. m. It was called to order by the late lamented Rev. William J. Simmons, D. D., President of the State University of Kentucky, who had been chiefly instrumental in having the Convention called. There were large delegations present from nearly all of the Southern States and a few from the East and West. Georgia sent only three delegates to this first meeting, while now she sends annually about one hundred. The three delegates from Georgia who attended the St. Louis meeting were the late Rev. E. K. Love, D. D., of Savannah, and the Revs. G. H. Dwelle and C. T. Walker, of Augusta. The Rev. Mr. Walker took a prominent part in the deliberations of the Convention, and served on the Committee on Permanent Organization. It was because of a wise, conservative and, considering the make-up of the Convention, bold stand that he took at this meeting, that he leaped, so to say, at one bound into national prominence as a fearless leader. It happened this way. On the second day of the meeting, one Rev. H. C. Bailey, of Florida, spoke on "Southern Ostracism." After abusing Southern white people for their treatment of the colored people, the Rev. Mr. Bailey said, among other things, that the Southern white Baptists were figureheads. Biding his time, the next day the Rev. Mr. Walker arose and addressing the chairman, said that he thought the statement made by the Rev. Mr. Bailey concerning the Southern white Baptists did them great injustice and ought not to be allowed to go unchallenged. Immediately every eye was turned toward the young champion from Georgia and there followed from him the most impassioned address of the entire meeting. He concluded by offering the following resolution, which, though vigorously opposed by many members of the Convention, was adopted by a good majority:

"WHEREAS, In the speech of H. C. Bailey, of Florida, yesterday, before this body, the statement was made that, as a whole, the Southern white Baptists were figureheads who do not follow Baptist teachings and who believe that there are separate heavens for white and colored people; and

"WHEREAS, Such as assertion does great injustice to the white Baptists of the South from the fact that they have many colored missionaries in the South paid by them to labor among our people; and

"WHEREAS, The Southern Baptist Convention at its meeting in January, 1886, in the city of Montgomery, Ala., passed a resolution to raise $10,000 to expend in mission work among the colored Baptists of the South; and

"WHEREAS, Such a statement as that referred to is likely to prove detrimental to the 800,000 colored Baptists of the South; therefore, be it

"*Resolved, First,* That this Convention does not endorse the statement of the brother referred to.

"*Resolved, Second,* That this Convention hears with the greatest gratification of the efforts now being made by the Southern Baptist Convention to expend $10,000 for missionary work among the colored people."

This resolution was published in many of the Southern newspapers and in all denominational organs; there was nothing but praise for the author. The Rev. Mr. Walker left home practically unknown outside of his own State; he returned one of the acknowledged leaders of the Baptist brotherhood of the country. The advertising he received from this incident doubtless in no small measure paved the way for his success in the East, whither he went a month later to solicit funds to assist him in his church work at Augusta.

Again, in 1889, at Indianapolis, while attending the National Baptist Convention, he added to his already growing reputation. Then, as in 1886, the Southern question was up for discussion. Many speakers indulged in wholesale abuse of the South; the white people of the South were pictured as heathen; they were vilified and maligned; race feeling ran high; there was great excitement. The Rev. Mr. Walker gained the floor and made an able speech counselling wisdom and moderation, and stating that he believed that the best element of white people in the South was trying to create such a public sentiment as would make lynching impossible. At any rate, he stated that the best thing for the colored people to do was to make the friendship of and seek the protection of the people among whom they lived. His speech acted like magic. Oil was poured on the troubled waters. Reason returned, and the resolutions under consideration were defeated. Again his name got into the newspapers; his speech was published

North and South; his name was on every tongue; some of the papers referred to him as "a strong man in a crisis."

It was at this meeting that he preached the Conventional sermon. It aroused and stirred all who heard it. At its conclusion, the late Rev. Dr. Simmons, the President of the Convention, walked over to the preacher, shook his hand, and said: "You have won your 'D. D.,' and I'll see that you get it." The following summer, true to his word, he had the trustees of the State University of Kentucky, of which he was President, to confer upon the Rev. Mr. Walker the honorary degree of "Doctor of Divinity," which he has worthily worn ever since.

From the beginning, Dr. Walker was one of the leading figures of the National Baptist Convention, and he is such to-day. For three years he was its Treasurer, and for many years was Vice President for Georgia. He is now Vice President for New York. He has attended every annual meeting since the beginning, without missing a single one. Not a partisan, not a factionist, not a stirrer up of strife among the brethren, not a division-maker, a man of peace, probably no man has a larger and more loyal following among the Negro Baptists of America than he has.

In June, 1898, he was appointed a Chaplain with the rank of Captain in the U. S. V., and assigned to duty with the Ninth Immunes. The appointment was made by the late President McKinley out of a list of more than 500 applicants. He secured a leave of absence from his Augusta church, and joined his regiment at San Luis, Cuba, about thirty miles inland from Santiago, in November, 1898. The regiment was only doing garrison duty at the time, the leading events in the Spanish-American War having already been long since concluded. During his absence, his church at Augusta was supplied by the Rev. Silas X. Floyd, at that time one of the Field Workers of the International Sunday School Convention.

The International Sunday School Convention is the largest and most important Sunday School organization in the world. It embraces in its membership the United States, the Dominion of Canada and South America, with corresponding representatives from Europe. It has a constituency of more than 23,000,000. It is sponsor for the International Lesson Series, which was inaugurated in 1872 by Mr. B. F. Jacobs, of Chicago, for many years past the able and honorable and venerable Chairman of the Executive Committee of the International Sunday School Convention. Closely associated with Mr. Jacobs in this great work have been, for many years, Dr. Geo. W. Bailey, of Philadelphia, the Treasurer and Chairman of the Finance Committee; Mr. John R. Pepper, of Memphis, Chairman of the Committee on Work Among the Colored People; Mr. John Wanamaker, of Philadelphia, and Mr. W. K. Crosby, of Wilmington, Del. The International Convention meets once every three years. At its last meeting, in 1899, in Atlanta, Ga., the Hon. Hoke Smith, Secretary of the Interior under Cleveland's second administration, was elected President, and Dr. Walker was elected one of the five Vice Presidents. He was unanimously presented for this place by the colored delegates present at the meeting, and these delegates represented many different denominations. It is an honor not lightly to be esteemed for a Negro to hold an office in such an important religious body.

During the past fifteen years, Dr. Walker has received calls from the following churches: First Baptist Church, Nashville,

Tenn.; the First Baptist Church, St. Louis; and the Second Baptist Church, Indianapolis. No one of these calls was accepted by the distinguished pastor. He preferred to remain with the people of Augusta.

CHAPTER XI.

CHAPLAIN U. S. V.

Dr. Walker joined his regiment, the Ninth Immunes, at San Luis, Cuba, the middle of November, 1898, and remained in the service for nearly two months. He did not find the service with the army very congenial, and resigned his commission to return to civil life. He remained with the army long enough, however, to get some notion of what army life means. He also learned much of Cuba, its climate and its peoples, and was able on his return to give a very interesting account of his trip, The following report is taken from the Augusta (Ga.) Chronicle, Jan. 5, 1899:

"Notwithstanding the rainy weather and the overcast night, it is probable that never before in its history was Tabernacle Baptist Church so overcrowded with people as on last night. It had been announced the day before that the pastor, Rev. C. T. Walker, D. D., recently with the Ninth Immune Infantry in Cuba, was to lecture on last night of his experience in that island.

"This notice was sufficient to pack the edifice up to the point of almost complete suffocation. Standing room was at a premium. Several hundred were turned away, and more than a hundred lingered in the yard on the stairways until the lecture closed. Possibly more than 1,200 persons heard the speaker.

"Dr. Walker, as is his custom, caught the audience from the beginning. He referred to the pleasure it gave him to be greeted by such a large gathering; he said it reminded him of the throng which welcomed him on his return from the Holy Land seven years ago. He said that there was great interest being manifested all over this country in Cuba and its people, especially because the Spanish yoke of oppression had been lifted from Cuba's neck, and the American flag now floated over that land, and the Cubans, so long oppressed, so long cruelly treated, were now free. He said he was glad it was so, because wherever the Stars and Stripes waved there the Gospel flag could not long be kept furled.

"He gave a brief account of his appointment last June by President McKinley, and, also, a short narrative of his journey to Santiago. His description of his entrance into the harbor of Santiago, passing Morro Castle, the sunken Mercedes, and the sunken Merrimac, was truly eloquent and brought down the house.

" 'Santiago,' he said, 'is one of the oldest cities in North America—older even than St. Augustine, Fla., having been founded in 1542. The streets are very narrow; the sidewalks are so narrow that two people cannot walk abreast; the city is extremely dirty; the water is unfit to drink, unless it is boiled; there are about 50,000 people in the city—15,000 of them white Cubans, and 35,000 of them black Cubans. Some of the people are intelligent, and some few engaged in business; but the vast majority of them are woefully ignorant and shiftless. Most of them at present are completely on the charity of the United States government. There are about 7,000 white soldiers in and around Santiago under General Leonard Wood, and about 3,000 colored soldiers out at San Luis, about 35 miles away—the Eighth Illinois, the Twenty-third Kansas and the Ninth Immune Infantry. The first two of these regiments have all colored officers from colonel down; my own regiment had all white officers excepting the lieutenants.

"He was particularly interested in San Juan Hill where, as he said, the battle was fought which decided the fate of Spain. He was particularly interested in it, because in that battle, the Twenty-fourth and Twenty-fifth Infantries, and the Ninth and Tenth Cavalries, all colored soldiers, led the charge, cut the barbed wire fence, captured the block-house, saved the Rough Riders, and added glory to the American nation and Negro race. He said he had stood on Bunker Hill, he had walked over the famous field of Waterloo, had crossed the valley of Ajalon where Joshua whipped five kings of the Amorites, and the Valley of Rephaim, where David conquered the Philistines, but he never was so inspired as he was when he stood on San Juan Hill, because there his own race was gallantly represented. At this the house thundered with applause.

"He said Cuba was a most beautiful country—more beautiful than even Germany or Switzerland. The soil is rich and fertile. Potatoes grow there as long as walking canes, and vegetation flourishes throughout the entire year. The weather he found to be extremely warm. December was like our June or July. No overcoats needed there. He thought the country was very unhealthy. The fever there is worse than Spanish bullets, and no one is 'immune' from it, not even the natives. The people are in a very low state of civilization, considered as a whole. In the rural districts, they do not live in houses, but 'shacks.' He had seen living in one little room, a husband and wife and five children, and a sow and six pigs. It is common for the people to live in the same room with horses, cows and hogs.

"He positively affirmed that, in his judgment, the Cubans were incapable of self-government. He found them to be very treacherous. They hate American soldiers, white and black. They thought America ought to have freed them and immediately given them their island to run to suit themselves. It was dangerous for any American to go alone at night; he would be killed by the Cuban machete.

"He mentioned the following as imperative needs of Cuba: churches, good schools, improved farming methods, and business enterprises. He thought that one thing that would greatly retard progress in Cuba was American prejudice, many examples of which he had observed while there. He said the American carried his prejudice wherever he went, and if American proscription along race lines was carried to Cuba, where such a thing had never been known, it would be an unhappy day for the island.

"In closing, he spoke of his success as chaplain. He had more than 100 converts, and had a baptism for three successive Sundays. His concluding words were a pathetic description of a scene which took place at one of his baptisms when one of the soldiers marched down to the water, singing:

> 'Ho, my comrades, don't you want to go?
> Let's go down to Jordan, hallelu.'

"At the close he showed many interesting relics, which he brought home with him. He had four Spanish rifles, a large supply of Mauser bullets, one machete, some cocoa, some coffee, some walking sticks made of iron wood, a Cuban pitcher, etc."

The same night the above address was delivered, resolutions were unanimously adopted thanking the speaker for his interesting address and expressing the pleasure of the people at his safe return. Thanks were also tendered the late President McKinley for appointing Dr. Walker as chaplain with the rank of captain in the U. S. V.

CHAPTER XII.

AS AN EVANGELIST.

Mention has been made in a preceding chapter of the fact that Dr. Walker has been very successful in the field of evangelistic work. In speaking of his work as an evangelist, let it be understood at the outset that the only limitation that has been put upon his efforts in evangelism has been due to the fact that all along he has been a stated pastor and has only given such time to evangelistic campaigns as he could spare from an unusually busy pastorate. Yet even with this limitation he has been very successful in evangelistic work, though he has not been able, for the reason stated, to accept scores of invitations from great cities to serve the Lord by conducting revival services.

He has the calling, the spirit, the gift, the courage, the directness, the sympathy, the faith, the fervor, and the flexibility of the true evangelist. What gives him his greatest preaching power is the enthusiastic warmth and impulsiveness of his speech both in matter and manner. Another thing that adds to the attractiveness of his meetings is the singing. Unlike most of the world's greatest preachers, he is a great singer. It has been often said of him that he can out-preach any man, and then, without stopping, put in and out-sing any man. It is beyond the power of man to describe an audience of four or five thousand colored people engaged in a service of song. In addition to the Gospel Hymns and Revival Songs, the colored people always use the old time Negro Spirituals, sometimes called Plantation Songs, and in the rendition of these last the colored people are inimitable. With Dr. Walker leading the singing in stentorian notes and the multitude joining in, its worth a day's journey of any man's life to witness the sight. To be understood, to be appreciated, it must be seen and heard.

At sometime or other, during the past twenty years, revival services have been held by Dr. Walker in every important city in Georgia without exception. It will be unnecessary to speak of each meeting. The first "big meetings" that gave him anything like a national standing as a recognized leading revivalist were held in Kansas City, Mo. The papers gave large space daily to the accounts of his meetings. This was in 1892, soon after his return from the Holy Land. During the progress of these meetings, invitations came to him to go to St. Louis, San Francisco, and Chicago to continue the good work. As much as he desired to do so, he was compelled to return to his church at Augusta, after five weeks of hard work, in which many hundreds were saved. In 1894, Dr. Walker was invited to New York City to take part in the great religious campaign inaugurated there during that year. The meetings were held during March and April. He remained for three weeks. He spoke at the Antioch Baptist Church, 352 W. 35th Street; St. Mark's M. E. Church, 139 W. 48th Street; Niblo's Garden, Broadway, near Prince Street; the Academy of Music, Metropolitan Hall, near Macy's, and at other points under assignment of the Metropolitan Association. He was associated with such men as the Rev. A. C. Dixon, the Rev. Ernest Lyon, the Rev. Granville Hunt, Mr. Arthur Crane, Leonard Weaver, Mr. Theodore Bjorksten, Mr. and Mrs. George C. Stebbins, the Rev. D. J. Burrell, and others. The following is taken from the New York Tribune concerning those meetings:

"The most unique figure in the present evangelistic campaign is, without a doubt, the Rev. Dr. Walker, of Georgia, who is better known as the 'Black Spurgeon.' This preacher has been working principally among the members of his own race in the course of his stay in New York, and has made many converts of the attendants at the meetings in Antioch Baptist Church and in St. Mark's M. E. Church. Dr. Walker is a man who would attract attention anywhere. He has strong features and his voice, although deep, has a remarkably winning intonation. His manner is eloquent, and in preaching Christ he follows closely the life of the Master, and illustrates his remarks by vivid descriptive phrases."

The column from which this is taken is headed "The Black Spurgeon's Work — Many Negroes Uplifted by His Eloquent Words—Part Which Dr. Walker is Taking in the Evangelical Services—His Attractive Personality."

The New York Sun said:

"'The Black Spurgeon' met with great success in his work in this city. He is a large and powerful man, with a deep voice, but what gives him his greatest preaching power is the earnestness he displays in matter and manner. Dr. Walker aroused a religious feeling which is finding expression in daily meetings. In St. Mark's, three meetings are held each day. The special aim of the revival has been to bring the young into the church, and to reclaim backsliders."

The New York Times, the New York Press, the New York Independent and other papers spoke of the "Black Spurgeon" and his work in New York at this time.

The following account of one of the Metropolitan noon-day meetings is taken from Sabbath Reading, a religious paper:

" 'Showers of Blessing,' was the opening hymn at a Metropolitan meeting a few days ago; and the reports of this and other meetings indicate that showers of blessing have indeed been falling. After several hymns had been sung, the Rev. Mr. Hunt led in prayer; Mr. Spencer sang touchingly the hymn, "My Son, Give Me Thine Heart.' Mr. Arthur Crane then spoke a short while. Miss Anna Parks rendered a solo on a cornet, 'When the Sea Gives up its Dead.' Dr. Walker, of Augusta, Ga., who is called the 'Black Spurgeon,' was introduced. He spoke in a voice tremulous with emotion and enthusiasm, and the audience gave him their close attention, that not a word might be lost. Opening the Bible, he read the first seven verses from Luke 5. 'There are four things to learn from this lesson,' he said; 'first, failure; second, faith; third, fullness; fourth, fellowship. These disciples had had a night of fruitless toil Jesus was not with them. They were fishermen and were plying their usual vocation on the lake, but they hadn't met with success. That was failure. In the morning, Jesus came along with a great crowd of people, and he asked Peter to lend him his ship for a pulpit, so that he might preach to the people. Peter did so, and to reward him for his courtesy, Jesus told him to launch out. Now, that seemed a foolish thing to do, because Peter and the others had been fishing all night, and hadn't caught one fish, and Jesus knew it; but he wanted to teach them a lesson of faith and obedience, as well as to reward them.

It's just like Jesus. He always does reward us right away, and he is continually paying us for what we do. The disciples took Jesus at his word: That was faith. And you know the story, how they let down the nets and drew in so many that the nets broke. That was fullness. Jesus always honors faith, even when it is mixed with ignorance and superstition. Seeing their companions at a distance with their empty boat, the disciples called them to come and share the fish with them. That was fellowship. The Lord intends that each of us shall share our joys with others. While this mighty tidal wave of religion is sweeping over the country, this is a good time for you to come to God and bring your friends with you. Jesus blesses us so that we might bless others. As he is exemplified in our conduct, so shall we win souls. Are there none here to-day who wish this Christ to come into their souls to be their own, their personal Saviour?' Several raised their hands for prayer, and the speaker said, 'Thank God.' "

Since 1894, Dr. Walker has held successful meetings in Galveston, Texas; Houston, Texas; Kansas City, St. Louis, Boston, Philadelphia, Nashville, Louisville and Atlanta. The last great meeting in Atlanta was held in April, 1897. The meetings commenced in Friendship Baptist Church, W. Mitchell St., of which the Rev. E. R. Carter, D. D., is the pastor. The interest increased so rapidly, and the number that came was so large that the meetings had to be transferred to the auditorium in Exposition Park, which before that had been made famous by meetings held by Sam Jones, and later by D. L. Moody. He crowded the great hall, with a seating capacity of nearly 8,000 souls, from the start. There probably has never been just such a meeting on the American continent as the one held in Atlanta at that time. It was attended by the white people as well as by the black people. At more than one service there were more than a thousand whites present—some of them representing the wealth and culture and refinement of Atlanta. Ministers, lawyers, members of the city council, the mayor and his wife, the merchants and bankers—all came out to hear the "Black Spurgeon." And the white people were just as eager, and some of them just as emotional in their worship as were the colored people. Many whites stood for prayer along with colored people; many were bathed in tears during the preaching; many of them testified for Jesus in the testimonial meetings; many were helped; some were saved. At the close of each meeting, the most prominent people would not think of leaving the building before shaking hands with the great preacher. Speaking of this meeting, the Atlanta Constitution said:

"The Negroes of Atlanta are stirred up over the wonderful religious revival that has been going on in the Friendship Baptist Church for the past two weeks. The success of the meeting has been unparalleled, and more religious enthusiasm has been aroused in the two weeks that the meetings have been running than has been felt in this city in years. The meetings are being conducted by the Rev. Charles T. Walker, 'the colored Spurgeon.' He is assisted by Rev. E. R. Carter, the regular pastor. Every night, thousands are turned away from the church on W. Mitchell St., and the building is always crowded with people long before the hour of service. Rev. Walker is proving as great a drawing card among the colored people as Sam Jones did among the whites. He attracts fully as large crowds and his preaching is drawing fully as many people into the church as Sam Jones' meeting—if not more.

Dr. Walker is pastor of the Tabernacle Baptist Church at Augusta, and is regarded as one of the leading colored preachers in the country. He attracts large crowds by his preaching wherever he goes, and his meetings are always attended by wonderful outbursts of religious enthusiasm."

In 1899, Dr. Walker again held meetings in Kansas City. The following is taken from the Kansas City Star, April, 1899:

"Many a white man would be glad to have the eloquence, the command of language and the power of thought that Rev. Dr. C. T. Walker, the 'Black Spurgeon,' displayed in his sermon to a great crowd of colored people in the Second Baptist Church, Tenth and Campbell Sts., last night. He is one of the best colored speakers ever heard in Kansas City.

"The Rev. Walker's home is in Augusta, Ga. He is so well thought of by the prominent people of his city that when the mayor died yesterday, he received several telegrams asking him to come and attend the funeral. He may return home to-day, but may decide to remain longer.

"Every seat in the large auditorium of the new colored church was occupied when he ascended the pulpit steps last night, and long rows of black faces looked down at him from the balcony.

"Dr. Walker is a man of perhaps forty or more. He is of medium size; although his face is as black as a stove pipe, he says he never drinks coffee because it is deleterious to the complexion. His features are prominent, he has a sharp mustache and a short head. His voice is not exceedingly strong, but clear and well modulated.

"His sermons are sententious and epigrammatic. They abound in original and striking observations, and his gestures, though not graceful, are spontaneous.

"'Men talk a great deal of the perplexing problems that confront humanity to-day,' he said. 'But if men would put the Bible into practice, there will be no problems. That book is statesmanship as well as religion, and it not only teaches the fatherhood of God, but the universal brotherhood of man.'

"The subject of his sermon was 'Christ the supreme object of worship.' In referring to God's plan of salvation, he said: 'So many say they failed to understand the plan and sometimes wondered why the Almighty did not take man into his confidence just a little bit in arranging it. But it wouldn't have done. In this day, when there are so many trusts and combines, salvation would have been bought up and cornered and monopolized until only the rich could get at it, if man had had anything to do with it. As some rhymester has said:

"'If religion was a thing that money could buy,
The rich would live and the poor would die.'"

"One of the characteristics of 'the Black Spurgeon's' style is his fund of illustrative anecdotes. He used one of these to show that man cannot read the Bible without feeling instinctively that Christ was divine, relating a conversation supposed to have taken place between Napoleon and Gen. Bertrand on the Island of St. Helena. When the latter expressed his opinion that Christ was only a man, Napoleon stopped him, and said: 'No, General Bertrand, I know men. But I never knew one like Christ. He had that in Him that no man ever had. He was divine. His army—soldiers of the cross—are now marching on through ages to victory. But who, general, think you, is marshalling any forces for me? In a year or two I shall die and be no more, and my name will be forgotten. But his name will live forever.'

"'Col. Ingersoll and Gen. Lew Wallace were once taking a ride together,' the speaker said, 'when Wallace informed his companion that he intended to write a book tearing the mask from the face of Christ and showing Him to have been but human. Ingersoll told him that he was the very man to write such a book and commended the idea.' 'When Gen. Wallace prepared to write the book,' said the preacher, 'he first set about reading the New Testament carefully as a prerequisite. Before he had finished it, he convinced himself of his own error and wrote Ben Hur instead.'

"'Over and over again,' continued the speaker, 'I have read of the Pharisee who, after recounting his virtues, thanked God that he was not like other men. And I have often wondered who this Pharisee was like. He was not like God, and he was not like the publican—he must have been like the devil.'

"Dr. Walker dealt sanctification a blow in declaring that such a thing as perfection was impossible to man. Man was intended to grow unceasingly into Christian strength.

"'The Lord's our judge,' he said, 'the Lord is our King; the Lord is our law-giver—the judicial. The executive and legislative combined in one.'

"But it is his pictures of the hereafter, of the hosts of saints marching up to glory, that the Black Spurgeon excels. Then it is that his voice is raised and his body sways back and forth as he adds stroke after stroke to the grand scene, and marshals phalanx after phalanx of moral heroes in Miltonic array, moving on with steady tread, glittering, triumphant, to the gates of heaven. In the course of a bit of description of this kind, near the close of his sermon, shouts went up from every quarter of the church and the audience was worked up to a high pitch of religious frenzy and exaltation.

" 'I hear the tread of the feet of the great host,' he said, 'tramp, tramp, tramp, they come. Like the angel whose wings John, in his vision saw released, they are not retarded by polar snows nor equatorial heat.'

" 'On they come—tramp tramp, tramp, shoulder to shoulder, wheel to wheel, charger to charger; onward they march—company after company, cavalcade after cavalcade, thousands upon thousands and millions upon millions, marching, marching, marching, on through the ages and forever. The church of God is going home to Zion. Ah! friends many are waiting there for you! That mother that lies buried beneath the sod, that little son or daughter, that sister, that brother—they are waiting and calling for you. Be of good courage, they say. They are not far away; they see your struggles; they know your temptations.'

" Then when the emotion of the audience began to find vent in shouts, the speaker lowered his voice and shifted to another line of attack, gradually working upon the feelings of his hearers again until he was again compelled to let up."

It is not necessary to prolong this chapter. The record of service done in the Master's Vineyard by Dr. Walker is one to be proud of. He has led more than 8,000 persons to Christ, has baptized and received into the membership of the church more than 3,500, and has not missed preaching the glorious Gospel of the blessed Christ but four Sundays in twenty-four years—twice on account of sickness, and twice on account of being at sea.

CHAPTER XIII.

LEAVES AUGUSTA—GOES TO NEW YORK.

In the month of June, 1899, a unanimous call was extended to Dr. Walker to become Pastor of the Mt. Olivet Baptist Church, 161 W. 53d St., New York City. Soon after, by invitation, he visited New York to confer with the officers of the church with regard to the work. The meeting between the pastor-elect and the officers was satisfactory in every way, and the former signified his intention of accepting the call. Returning to Augusta, he presented his resignation as pastor of Tabernacle Baptist Church, to take effect on the 1st day of October, 1899, on which date he proposed to enter upon work in New York City.

It is putting the matter mildly to say that the members of the Tabernacle Church and the people of Augusta were in a frenzy. Mass meetings were held, protest after protest was filed by various civic and benevolent organizations, the newspapers rebelled, the Tabernacle Baptist Church voted to add $50.00 per month to his salary, the whole city was literally stirred in an effort to get him to reconsider his acceptance of the New York invitation and withdraw the resignation he had tendered as Pastor of Tabernacle Church. These efforts were unavailing, because Dr. Walker said that he felt moved of the Spirit to go to New York. As a compliment to the pastor, the Tabernacle Baptist Church refused to accept his resignation, and passed resolutions to the effect that he be left free to go to New York if he desired, but stipulating expressly that he could return at any date to the pastorate of the Tabernacle Church, which he had founded, and of which he had

TABERNACLE BAPTIST CHURCH, AUGUSTA, FOUNDED BY DR. CHARLES T. WALKER.

been the able, successful and beloved leader for 14 years. With this understanding, the Rev. Silax X. Floyd was unanimously elected as Pastor of the Tabernacle Baptist Church, and installed as Pastor on Tuesday night, Sept. 26, 1899.

The following account of Dr. Walker's last Sunday night with his Augusta church is taken from the Augusta (Ga.) Chronicle of Sept. 25, 1899:

"Last night Dr. C. T. Walker preached his farewell sermon at Tabernacle Baptist Church. The church was packed to overflowing. A Chronicle reporter called soon after the service commenced, and found great crowds going away, unable to gain admission.

"The service commenced by singing, 'Come, ye disconsolate,' the hymn being read by the Rev. Silas X. Floyd, A. M., pastor-elect of Tabernacle Church. Prayer was offered by Bishop R. S. Williams, of the C. M. E. Church.

"Dr. Walker used for a text Acts 20:32, 'And now, brethren, I commend you to God, and to the word of his grace, which is able to build you up, and to give you an inheritance among all them which are sanctified."

"In his opening remarks, the speaker referred to the fact that in the 20th chapter of Acts the apostle Paul was delivering his farewell message to the elders of Ephesus. Concerning himself, the apostle had been desirous all along of two things. One was that he might be faithful, and the other was that he might finish well. The apostle commended the Ephesians to God—to God's providence, to God's protection, to God's word. He commended them in this way for their edification and for their glorification.

"Then leaving the text, he delivered some very pathetic and helpful parting words to his congregation. Among other things he urged them to be a united people; he plead with them to stand together and to uphold the hands of the young man who had been called to succeed him; he urged them to be industrious, progressive, self-respecting and self-reliant; with much eloquence he called upon them to be interested in all the affairs of their race—he appealed to them to be law-abiding and to make themselves a credit to the race and to the city of Augusta and not a disgrace.

"Parting words were also spoken to the officers of the church. Parting thanks were expressed to the church, to the sinners, to the citizens, white and colored, who had stood by him and made his success possible.

"In closing he gave a brief summary of his 14 years work in this city. During that time he has baptized at his church over 1,400 people erected a handsome brick church, bought an 'Old Folks' Home,' the church and home valued at over $20,000, and done many other things of which he did not speak. Many of the congregation were shedding tears at the close of the service. The parting hymn was 'God be with you till we meet again.'"

The Mount Olivet Baptist Church was organized March 10, 1878. Rev. Daniel W. Wisher was its first pastor. The church had its place of worship in West 26th St., until 1885. In that year, by the help of generous white Baptist friends and the Baptist City Mission Society, they were enabled to purchase the splendid edifice in W. 53rd St., valued then at $130,000, in which they still worship. During the pastorate of Rev. D. W. Wisher, or from 1878 to 1899, the church paid on its debt, $39,000, of this $18,000 were given by Mr. John D. Rockefeller, Mr. W. M. Isaacs, Mr. James Pyle, Mr. W. A. Caldwell, Mr. Samuel S. Constant, Mrs. Nathan Bishop, Mr. J. A. Bostick, Mr. J. F. Coney, Mr. B. F. Judson, Mr. R. Parker and others through the Baptist City Mission Society.

In 1897 during the heated political campaign in New York City, the Rev. D. W. Wisher saw fit to side with Tammany Hall in the city election, and, it is said, went so far as to preach a sermon in which he advocated Tammany's claims and advised his members to vote the Tammany ticket. As a result of this new departure, great opposition to the Rev. Mr. Wisher sprang up in the church, and for nearly two years there was an unseemly church wrangle by which the church was finally divided into two factions, known as the "Wisherites" and the "Anti-Wisherites."

It would be offensive to go into details. After a series of court trials the "Anti-Wisherites" triumphed. The Rev. Mr. Wisher was deposed in 1899, and his followers left the church.

It was then that the Mt. Olivet Baptist Church commenced to look for a new leader. The Rev. Chas. S. Morris, D. D., of Boston, Mass., was called to lead the church temporarily. After prayer and deliberation, the church looked to Georgia, its eye fell on the "Black Spurgeon," and he was invited to become pastor of the church. As already stated, after conference with those in authority, Dr. Walker decided to accept the new charge. At first his friends throughout the nation felt that he was making a mistake, the church already divided, the people who had kept up with the "church war" (so far as they could keep up with it from the newspaper reports) felt that it would be impossible for any human being to reunite the membership. But Dr. Walker undertook the task, trusting in the Lord. He succeeded from the day he took charge, the first Sunday in October, 1899. From that day to this there has not been the slighest friction in the church, and the membership has increased from about 430 to more than 1,800 in the short space of two years and four months. Besides, it is said by

MT. OLIVET BAPTIST CHURCH, WEST FIFTY THIRD STREET, NEW YORK CITY, N. Y.

those competent to give correct opinions in the matter that from the beginning he has preached to the largest regular congregations of any man in New York City, white or black.

The second Sunday in March, 1900, he baptized 184 converts at one time, which is the record for New York City, and perhaps for the country. It was such an unusual spectacle that all the New

York newspapers gave large space to a report of the baptism and the Associated Press sent a long account of it throughout the length and breadth of the country. At the night service the pastor gave the hand of fellowship to 408 members.

The second Sunday in March, 1901, he had another large baptism, in which 95 were baptized, and the second Sunday in February, 1902, more than 100 were baptized into the fellowship of the Mt. Olivet Baptist Church. In all there have been more than 1,400 added to the church under his administration, 700 by baptism and about 700 by letters and Christian experiences. These last are usually called backsliders. They are persons who were at one time members of Baptist churches in other places, but who have been in New York, some ten, some fifteen and some twenty years, without connecting themselves with any churches, while at the same time they lost their identity with the churches where they formerly were members. Dr. Walker has reclaimed hundreds of these, and they are making good church members.

Financially his success with the church has been remarkable. In round numbers, he has raised for all purposes, $25,000. He has kept up the interest on the church debt and paid $2,500 on the principal. He has raised $3,000 for the Colored Men's Branch Y. M. C. A.; $2,500 for Home and Foreign Missions, and more than $2,000 for various charities. Among the regular contributors to the church at the present time are Mrs. Geo. Lewis, Mr. W. R. A. Martin, and Mr. James W. Talcott.

The Mt. Olivet Baptist Church is a commodious structure, three stories high with a beautiful granite front. The first floor contains the trustees' room, library room, the deacon's room, one large dressing room, kitchen and Sunday School room and the lecture room—the library room and trustees' room, by means of folding doors, can be thrown into the lecture room. The second floor contains the main auditorium and the choir gallery with two large swinging galleries. The third floor contains the pastor's study and room for committees, choir practice, etc. Following is the list of present officers of Mt. Olivet Baptist Church:

DEACONS OF MT. OLIVET BAPTIST CHURCH.

Wm. Moore, Chairman. Born in Hertford County, N. C., in 1855. Joined Mt. Olivet Baptist Church in 1881. Made deacon in 1882. Served for several years on the Advisory Board.

Fleming W. Jackson, Vice Chairman. Born in New Kent County, Va., in 1836. Joined Mt. Olivet Baptist Church in 1879 by letter from Second Baptist Church, Richmond, Va. Licensed to preach by Joy Street Baptist Church, Boston, Mass., and also by the Mt. Olivet Baptist Church. Served for five years on the Advisory Board of the Mt. Olivet Baptist Church and for the past four years has been a deacon.

J. A. Gardener, born in Shirley, near Richmond, Va., in 1846. Joined Mt. Olivet Baptist Church when it was organized in 1878. Has been a member of the board of deacons 22 years.

G. P. Webb. Born in Orange County, Va., Oct. 7, 1850. Joined Mt. Olivet Baptist Church in 1878. Been a member of the Board of deacons since 1885. Deacon Webb is also Vice President Board of Trustees.

Robert H. Jones. Born in 1850 in Petersburg, Va. Joined Mt. Olivet Baptist Church in 1885. Became deacon in 1898.

Herbert S. Royal. Born in Nottoway County, Va., Oct. 31,

1858. Joined Mt. Olivet Baptist Church in 1884. Served as an usher for three years; member of the Advisory Board for two years, and made a deacon in 1894.

David Grant. Born in 1848, in Marengo County, Ala. Joined Mt. Olivet Baptist Church in 1882; made a deacon in 1900.

John L. Walters. Born April 3, 1862, in Accomac County, Va. Joined Mt. Olivet Baptist Church in 1885. Served on Advisory Board for several years. Made a deacon in 1898. Deacon Waters is, also, Assistant Superintendent of the Sunday School.

General Grant Stephens. Born in Newbern, N. C., March 15, 1870. Joined Mt. Olivet Baptist Church in 1895. Made a deacon in 1900.

A. J. Campbell, Born in Nottoway County, Va., April 20, 1857. Joined Mt. Olivet Baptist Church in 1887. Made a deacon in 1900.

W. H. Holloway.

Samuel Swann.

TRUSTEE BOARD.

W. H. Jones, President; Henry Darnell, Treasurer; Cyrus Henry Trent, Secretary; James Wells, Assistant Secretary; Deacon G. P. Webb, Vice President; J. E. Taylor, Frank Youngblood, P. F. Comey (white), W. H. J. Innis (white).

OTHER OFFICERS.

J. E. Decker, Church Clerk; Prof. J. S. Brown, Assistant Clerk; J. F. Comey (white), Treasurer; Wesley Norman, Superintendent of Sunday School; Deacon J. L. Walters, Assistant Superintendent of Sunday School; B. H. Green, President B. Y. P. U.:

Samuel Tabb, President Young People's Literary Society; Mrs. Charity Jones, President of the C. T. Walker Volunteer Club; Mrs. Clarence Robinson, President of the United Tribes (auxiliary to the Y. M. C. A.); Deacon F. W. Jackson, President of the Co-workers; Prof. A. C. Fletcher, Chorister; Madam V. E. Hunt Scott, Organist; John Collie, Sexton; Robert Washington, Assistant Sexton.

CHAPTER XIV.

COLORED MEN'S BRANCH Y. M. C. A.

Dr. Walker had not been a resident of New York six months before he turned his attention to the organization of a Young Men's Christian Association for colored young men. He had looked around and had found no place for hundreds and hundreds of colored young men to spend their evenings and Sundays, except in saloons, dives and brothels. Without consulting anybody, though he was at the headquarters of the International Y. M. C. A., he called a public meeting at Mt. Olivet Baptist Church, and organized a Y. M. C. A. Nearly every colored pastor in the city, regardless of denomination, became interested in the movement, and gave Dr. Walker almost undivided support. Money was raised, a building at 132 West 53rd Street was leased for one year, temporary officers were elected, and Dec. 18, 1900, application was made to the Y. M. C. A. of New York City for membership as one of the regular branches. The application was received and acted on favorably, and since then the Colored Men's Branch has been oneof the regular branches of the City Association. In January, 1901, Mr. Walter C. Coles, of Aiken, S. C., was appointed Secretary of the Colored Men's Branch and immediately took charge of the work. He served only one year, having been summoned to

REV. WALTER C. COLES, DECEASED EX-SECRETARY OF COLORED Y. M. C. A., NEW YORK CITY, N. Y.

report to God, Saturday, Jan. 4th, 1902. The following obituary notice is taken from the Presbyterian Herald, of New York City:

"Rev. Walter C. Coles died suddenly of typhoid fever, at his home, 331 West 59th Street, Saturday, January 4th, 1902. Mr. Coles was the oldest son of the Rev. William R. and Mrs. Coles, of Aiken, S. C. He was a graduate both of the College and Theological Departments of Biddle University, N. C.

"It was in the Biddle University where Mr. Coles developed his great power as a 'Fisher of Men.' He organized the University men, whom he held together by his shrewd method of dealing and his heart of love.

"He engaged in regular pastoral work at Nimrod, N. C. and Aiken, S. C.

"The Rev. Chas. T. Walker, D. D., came to New York as pastor of the Mt. Olivet Baptist Church in 1899.

"He at once began work among the men, organized a Colored Men's Branch of the Y. M. C. A. Within a year this organization had grown to be a great power for good. A secretary was needed. Walter Coles was the man. He was appointed Secretary of the Colored Men's Branch of the Y. M. C. A., 132 West 53rd Street, January 1901. He therefore served only one year.

"In September, 1901, he was ordained by the Presbytery of McClelland, in South Carolina, and was married to Miss Mattie Belk, of Greenville, in the same month and the happy couple came to New York to engage in their life work. But alas! How soon was he cut down. He had lived a full life. His work was done. His task ended.

"A memorial service was held in Mount Olivet Baptist Church, Sunday afternoon. The Colored Branch and the Ladies' Auxiliary were present in a body. Among the speakers were Chairman Walker, the Rev. Dr. William H. Brooks, Pastor of St. Mark's Methodist Episcopal Church; the Rev. Hutchins C. Bishop, Pastor of St. Philip's Protestant Episcopal Church; Vice Chairman G. W. Allen, Messrs. A. S. Newman, representing the Board of Directors; E. W. Booth, General Secretary; B. M. Lewis, of the East Side Branch, and Mr. Bannister of the Harlem Branch. The

REV. T. J. BELL,

SECRETARY COLORED Y. M C. A., NEW YORK CITY.

chancel was filled with a large number of handsome floral pieces. Sunday evening the remains were carried to Aiken, accompanied by Mr. Coles's wife, mother and H. C. Dugas.' "

The death of Mr. Coles was a serious blow to the work, but the work is still being carried on in the name of the Lord. Rev. Thomas J. Bell, of Altamaha, Ga., a graduate of Atlanta University and Hartford Theological Seminary, has been appointed to succeed the late Mr. Coles, and will enter upon his duties April 1, 1902. The Association has now $2,000 on hand for a building fund and more than $500 in the treasury for current expenses. Too much cannot be said in praise of the efforts of the United Tribes in raising money for the Y. M. C. A. The Tribes are a company of women of the Mt. Olivet Baptist Church, which serves as an auxiliary to the Y. M. C. A. Deacon Fleming Jackson is President of the United Tribes. By means of fairs, the tribes have raised for the work of the Colored Men's Branch more than $3,000. Dr. Walker has found them an invaluable auxiliary.

The present officers are the following Board of Managers:

Rev. C. T. Walker, D. D., Chairman; Geo. W. Allen, Vice Chairman; John A. Robinson, Secretary; J. F. Comey, Treasurer; Rev. P. Butler Thompkins, Rev. W. H. Brooks, Rev. W. D. Cook, Rev. H. C. Bishop, Mr. Henry Darnell, John S. Brown, Jr., E. P. Roberts, Walter Handy, Anderson Ferrall, Jr., A. S. Newman, Edmund W. Booth, A. B. Cooper, Rev. W. L. Hubbard.

Special mention should be made of a life-size oil painting of Dr. Walker, the founder and Chairman of the Branch, given to the Colored Men's Branch by the Ladies' Auxiliary Society of Mt. Olivet Baptist Church. This painting adorns the walls of the Colored Men's Branch.

Special mention, also, should be made of the invaluable services rendered Dr. Walker by his private Secretary, Mr. Henry C. Dugas, of Augusta, Ga. Mr. Dugas went to New York with Dr. Walker, in 1899, and continued his right-hand man until October, 1901. At that time, Dr. Walker was thinking about going South again to live, and, with his characteristic large-heartedness, he looked about to place Mr. Dugas in some good position. Through friends he was able to place Mr. Dugas as one of the Secretaries of Mr. George Foster Peabody, the millionaire banker, philanthropist and publicist. Mr. Dugas has given prefect satisfaction in his new

HENRY C. DUGAS,

FORMER SECRETARY OF DR. WALKER, NOW PERSONAL SECRETARY FOR GEORGE FOSTER PEABODY.

station. He is a graduate of the Oberlin Business College, is an accomplished stenographer and typewriter, steady in his habits, modest and unassuming in his general deportment, and indefatigable in the performance of his duties. Since Mr. Dugas left Dr. Walker, the duties of private Secretary have been ably and successfully performed by Miss Annie L. Connelly, of New York City.

The most significant fact in connection with the Colored Y. M. C. A. is that all efforts to organize an association among the colored men of New York failed until Dr. Walker came to the city and applied his heart and mind and energy to the task. The instant success of the movement attracted wide-spread attention, and long after he is dead, Dr. Walker will be known in history as the founder of the first Colored Y. M. C. A. in New York City. The work is bound to grow and increase with the years that are to come. It is confidently predicted that within a year, the Colored Men's Branch will have a finely located building that will cost upwards of $50,000.

CHAPTER XV.

CALLED TO AUGUSTA AGAIN.

Rev. Silas X. Floyd resigned the pastorate of Tabernacle Church, Augusta, Ga., Nov. 15, 1900. The resignation was not accepted by the church, but Rev. Mr. Floyd decided to leave the pastorate and took his departure Jan. 1, 1901. The Tabernacle Church, being now without a leader, looked to its founder and first pastor for aid and comfort. In June, 1901, a unanimous call was tendered to Dr. Walker to return to his old work. Dr. Walker greatly loved the people of his old church, and felt grateful toward them for standing by him so loyally in his earlier years when he was not so prominent, and felt it to be his duty to return to them. He notified the Mt. Olivet Baptist Church of his intention to leave New York, Oct. 1, 1901, and take up again his old work at Augusta. There was a spontaneous protest from the whole church and from the entire city, as may be easily seen from the files of the newspapers of the metropolis. The city was up in arms; the church passed resolutions, imploring Dr. Walker to remain in New York, and many other organizations did likewise.

The strong protest against his leaving New York culminated in a mass meeting, held in Mt. Olivet Baptist Church, New York City, Wednesday night, Nov. 6, 1901. The following circular, sent out by the church and citizens, will illustrate the vigorous effort made to keep Dr. Walker in New York City:

"Mass meeting of the officers, members and the congregation of Mt. Olivet Baptist Church, Rev. Dr. Charles T. Walker, Pastor, to be held in the church, West 53rd St., on Wednesday evening, Nov. 6, 1901, at 8 o'clock.

"The purpose of this meeting is to give expression to our great love, respect, affection and regard for Rev. Dr. Charles T. Walker, and to show him how strong our desire is to have him remain among us as our spiritual comforter, friend and adviser.

"We not only desire him to remain with us, but we also desire to show him the sincerity and strength of this desire.

"We desire to show him how much we appreciate his Christian character, his polished sermons, his matchless eloquence, his bright and versatile intelligence, his noble manhood, his genial and kindly spirit, his undying loyalty to his people, and all those good qualities which have so endeared him to our hearts, and which go to make the very highest and best of the Christian ministry.

"We want his people in Augusta, Ga., to learn from us how dear he is to us, and that we cannot and will not allow him to depart from among us, and to persuade them to give up all thoughts of inducing him to leave a field of usefulness to us as a race, which cannot well be filled by others (let them be who they may).

"Rev. Dr. Robert S. MacArthur, pastor Calvary Baptist Church, West 57th Street, will preside. Addresses will be made by Right Rev. William B. Derrick, Bishop of the A. M. E. Church; Dr. Cook, pastor Bethel A. M. E. Church; Dr. William H. Brooks, pastor of St. Mark's M. E. Church, F. R. Morse, assistant pastor Calvary Baptist Church, West 57th Street; Pierce B. Thompkins, pastor of St. James Church, West 32nd Street; Hutchins Bishop, pastor of St. Philip's Church; Dr. W. T. Dixon, Pastor Concord

Baptist Church, Brooklyn; John D. Rockefeller, Jr., James Alex. Williams, Consulting Physician and Inspector Department of Health, N. Y. City; F. V. C. Cato, Superintendent of the A. M. E. Church Sabbath School, and W. G. M. F., and A. M. S. of New York; W. R. Davis, Alexander Powell, Assistant Inspector Department of New York, G. A. R., and Past Commander Post 234; R. H. Hutchless, P. E. G. C. K. of T.; Winfield Jackson, President of Saloon Men's Protective Association, No. 1, of New York City; Alfred Christian, President of Bronx Republican Club, New York City; T. T. Fortune, Editor of New York Age; Wm. H. Randolph, Commander Post 234, Department of N. Y., G. A. R.; David Prime, James Mann, John R. Bradford, A. L. Askew, John H. Chase, Robert Franklin, Jeremiah Stewart, Robert P. Gilmore, Theodore Warren.

"Music under the direction of Albert C. Fletcher, Choirmaster of the church; Mme. V. E. Hunt Scott, Organist."

The meeting referred to in the above circular was carried out almost to the letter, and was said to have been the largest church meeting ever held in New York City. The following letter sent to the meeting by Rev. W. C. Bitting, pastor of one of the largest white churches in New York, is so very full and explicit that we give it space in this book.

"I would be sorry to see Mr. Walker leave our city. Our colored brethren have suffered horribly from incompetent and uneducated leaders in this city, and are suffering in the same way now, in many churches. What a well prepared man can do has been demonstrated by the pastorate of Mr. Walker. I wish that he could see his way to remain with us, and that the example of Mt. Olivet Church in calling and keeping an educated pastor

ROBERT STUART MACARTHUR, D.D.,
PASTOR CALVARY BAPTIST CHURCH, NEW YORK.

would be followed by all the other churches. We would have a different story to tell about our work if our colored brethren would not take up with pious and illiterate tramps. This will show you my feeling about Mr. Walker's work and continuance among us.

"It is a matter which I suppose he will settle between the Lord and himself, and I also honor him enough to believe that he does not need begging to keep him here if he sees it to be his duty to stay, and I also honor him enough to believe that he will go if he believes it to be his duty to go. I have not much heart to meddle with what must by nature be a matter between God and Mr. Walker. Neverthelsss, I earnestly hope he may see it to be his duty to stay and help not only Mt. Olivet, but all the other churches, and his race and the city by the continuance of what has been in many respects a remarkable ministry. Such a man ought to be allowed to have his own way.

"Yours sincerely,

"W. C. Bitting."

One speech made at the mass meeting is deserving of more than passing notice; it was delivered by Col. Alexander Powell, Past Commander Post 234, G. A. R. It reflected the opinion of all present. Extracts follow:

"I state my conviction to you and to my comrades of the Grand Army of the Republic, who are members of this church, by saying that Dr. Walker owes a duty to the members of this church which has so wonderfully prospered under him, that should be as sacred as the one he seeks to discharge in that far distant city of Augusta, Georgia. He has instilled into the hearts of all who have been so fortunate as to hear him preach, a clearer understanding of Christ crucified and the forgiveness of those who trespass against us; the work he bravely and uncomplainingly has done in the building up of the Young Men's Christian Association, together with his undying loyalty to us as a race, has not only touched the hearts of those who know him best, but has been felt far and wide. I know, too, something of the injustice he has suffered while doing the bidding of our Heavenly Father, but with a Christian spirit he has forgiven those who would spitefully use him, and prayed for those who wronged him.

"The gathering memories of olden days always gather about me as I cross the threshold of this church, and to-night more so than ever. The traveler standing in the beautiful Valley of Chamonix, at the base of Mont Blanc, fails to realize the stupendous height of that snow-capped peak, but when miles distant he turns back and beholds it towering far above its compeers, he recognizes its claim to be called the Monarch of Mountains.

"It is so with Dr. Walker. Now that his resignation has been placed in your hands, your judgments have matured and you realize the difficulties he has overcome, the Christian works he has accomplished, and the blessings he has brought to the people, his retention becomes precious and priceless to you.

"He is the beau ideal of a minister. His Christianity is the natural growth of his life. His fame as a preacher has come to him unsought, his administration of the finances of your church has been successful because it has been based on honesty. His achievements since he has been a resident of this imperial city compel admiration; they touch the finer chords of our nature. They inspire feelings akin to those we experience in listening to the grand strains of an oratorio. His success is not the success that makes fools admired and villains honest. It is not the success of accident, which bursts forth like a meteor and as suddenly disappears; it is not that acquired by selfishness, that is tinctured with envy, jealousy, hypocrisy, or refuses to lend a helping hand, but it has been a success that was established upon morals, worth, courage, justice and honor.

"Rev. Dr. Walker, I give you my hand, and I want you to understand, Sir, that when I give you my hand as Assistant Inspector of the Department of New York, Grand Army of the Republic, 78,599 of the boys who wore the blue in that memorable crisis are taking you by the hand and urging you to remain among us.

"The G. A. R. bids you remain. We wish that your life may be spared many years; that abundance, prosperity, and happiness may attend you and this church. This, I am sure, is not only the hearty wish of every one present, but also that of every colored man, woman and child from the Battery to the Spuyten Duyvil."

It is not to be doubted that the great interest shown by all classes in having Dr. Walker remain in New York had much to do with his subsequent decision.

Meanwhile the people of Augusta were not sleeping; they had a mass meeting, also, as the following circular will show:

"A mass meeting of the officers, members, friends and well-wishers of Tabernacle Baptist Church will be held in the church on Monday evening, November 18, 1901, at 8 o'clock. Ministers of all the denominations (white and colored), professional and business men, the presidents and prominent men of the fraternal and benevolent organizations, together with the political and prominent educational leaders of the city of Augusta, will be presten to join in the urgent request to Dr. Charles Thomas Walker not to alter his determination to resume his pastorate at Augusta, Ga.

"All citizens of Augusta and vicinity are invited to attend a mass meeting to be held at Tabernacle Baptist Church on Monday night, November 18, 1901.

"The object of this meeting is to give expression to our feelings regarding the return of Dr. C. T. Walker to the pastorate in this city, and to demonstrate the regard in which we hold him and the real need we feel for his presence.

"We desire to show the country the supreme regard in which we hold this man whose labors for the betterment of no race or clan, but of all humanity have made him a worthy servant of his Master and an able leader of the people.

"We want our brethren in New York City to feel that we desire not to take from them that which is theirs, but merely to claim our own. Under sufferance we have remained silent until this time, when we are forced by absolute necessity to call upon our metropolitan friends to return our Joseph to his brethren and our Moses to his people.

"Bishop R. S. Williams, of the C. M. E. Church, will preside.

"Addresses will be made by Rev. W. J. White, D. D., pastor Harmony Baptist Church; Rev. H. Seb. Doyle, M. A., pastor of Trinity C. M. E. Church; Rev. C. S. Wilkins, D. D., pastor Thankful Baptist Church; Rev. W. C. Gaines, pastor Bethel A. M. E. Church: Rev. D. S. Klugh, pastor Union Baptist Church; Rev. F. M. Hyder, pastor Christ Presbyterian Church; Rev. D. J. Flynn, pastor Congregational Church; Rev. S. X. Floyd, A. M., District Missionary American Baptist Publication Society;

Rev. J. W. Whitehead, pastor of Mt. Moriah Baptist Church; Rev G. W. Harrison, pastor Macedonia Baptist Church; Rev. R. J. Johnson; Rev. A. W. Wilson, pastor Hosanna Baptist Church; Rev. F. M. Hauser, pastor Woodlawn Baptist Church: Rev. Thomas Walker, Dr. George N. Stoney, Dr. W. T. Prichett, Dr. G. S. Burruss, Dr. N. A. Mixson, Dr. A. N. Gordon, Dr. R. C. Williams, P. H. Craig, Esq., Principal Nellieville School; A. W Wimberly, Esq., Collector Internal Revenue; G. J. Scott, Esq., President Union Relief Association; Prof. N. W. Curtright, Principal Walker Baptist Institute; Rev. G. H. Dwelle, pastor Springfield Baptist Church; Prof. A. R. Johnson, Principal Mauge Street School; Prof. I. Blocker, Principal Second Ward School; Dr. Geo. W. Walker, President Paine College; W. J. White, Jr., Associate Editor Georgia Baptist; L. E. Moseley, President Morning Stars of Benevolence; H. B. Sweet, President Brothers and Sisters of Love; John G. Williams, merchant; H. C. Young, merchant; F. M. Dugas, undertaker; A. J. Winter, President Painters' Union; R. R. Battey, wheelwright; H. D. Paschal, shoemaker; T. B. Newsome, tailor, and other citizens, white and colored. Music under the direction of Wesley Warren, Choirmaster, and Prof. W. H. E. Carter, Organist.

Thus, two churches, separated by more than 800 miles, were claiming and clamoring for the same man to serve them as pastor. The battle waged for many weeks, or until Dec. 1, 1901, when Dr. Walker decided to continue the pastorate of Mt. Olivet Church with an assistant pastor, keeping his headquarters in New York City, but, in obedience to the wishes of the Augusta church, he agreed to become the nominal pastor of Tabernacle Baptist Church. Under this arrangement, he is to visit the Southern church two or three times a year, and, in his absence, he is to supply the pulpit. This arrangement pleased all concerned, and, for the present, seems to be working well.

CHAPTER XVI.

EXTRACTS FROM SERMONS.

Wednesday, June 6, 1888, by appointment of the Missionary Baptist State Convention of Georgia, the Rev. Mr. Walker preached the opening sermon in honor of the one hundredth anniversary of the founding of the Negro Baptist Church in Georgia. The centennial exercises were conducted on a grand scale, running through ten days, and the fact that he was selected to preach the opening sermon shows the esteem in which he was held by his brethren. Following are some extracts from the sermon preached by the great leader and preacher at that time:

WHAT HATH GOD WROUGHT.

"'According to this time it shall be said, What hath God wrought.'—Numbers 23:23.

"We stand to-day upon an eminence from which we may take a retrospective view of a one hundred years' journey. This is a glorious day. We have come to celebrate the progress and triumphs of a century. We are here to speak of the vicissitudes through which we have passed, the conflicts we have encountered, the obstacles we have overcome, the success already attained, and the victories yet to be achieved. We are here to pass up and down the line of march from 1788 to 1888. Old fathers, worn and weary with burdens and cares of long and useful lives, their heads whitened by the frosts of many winters, infirm and superannuated, have come up to shake hands with the century, to bid God-speed to their brethren, and, like Simeon of old, to exclaim, 'Lord, now lettest thou thy servant depart in peace, for mine eyes have seen thy salvation.' Young men have come to get inspiration from a review of the work of the fathers and to return to their various fields stimulated, electrified and encouraged.

"We shall discuss, first, what God has wrought in the permanent establishment of His church. The founder of the true church is Jesus Christ. He is the Son of Abraham, according to the flesh, and He is also the Son of God. Two natures and three offices mysteriously meet his person. He is the foundation of the true church, the chief corner stone, the lawgiver in Zion. He has given us a kingdom which cannot be moved. He began in Asia to ride in the gospel chariot. He sent out twelve small boats at first. On the dav of Pentecost, 3,000 were added to the number. In 1630, He sent Roger Williams to America. In the spirit of his Master, he planted churches in New England, and the stone continued to roll until it reached the sunny South. In 1788, the oppressed, rejected and enslaved brother in black, for the first time in Georgia, lifted the Baptist flag under the leadership of Andrew Bryan. The handful of corn was sown not on the high, wild and rocky mountains, but on the seaboard; but the wind carried the seed to every part of Georgia and the barren rocks and sandy deserts became gardens of the Lord. From that handful of corn have sprung more than 1,500 churches, 500 ordained preachers, and 166,429 communicants. The little one has become a thousand. In the entire United States there are to-day more than 1,250,000 colored Baptists. I make bold to say here and now that the progress of the Baptists in this country has been due to the earnest, faithful and simple preaching of Christ crucified. The fathers in their preaching did not preach philosophy, nor did they strive to reach the people with rhetorical strains of eloquence, but they strove to reach the people by preaching the plain, old-fashioned, simple truths of the gospel. The gospel declared in its truth and simplicity will make Baptists.

"Third, we shall discuss what God has wrought for our race during this century. For our race, this century was one of hardship, oppression, persecution and sore trial. We were slaves; we had no moral training; no intellectual advantages during the greater part of this century and the two preceding; we were run by bloodhounds; sometimes whipped to death; we were sold from the auction block, husbands and fathers being separated from wives and children at the behest of some white man; we had to get a ticket to go to church; we had to get permission from some white man before we could join the church; we were outcasts. But all that has been changed. God was against slavery, and in his own time and way He removed the foul blot from the national escutcheon. Emancipated without a dollar, without education, without friends and without competent leaders, like Hagar and Ishmael, we were turned out to die. But despite all obstacles, the Negro in Georgia has to-day $10,000,000 worth of property and has proven himself worthy of citizenship. We have thousands of children in our public schools. Our men will be found in the law, in the practice of medicine, in legislative halls, among teachers and professors, on the list of authors, skilled musicians, journalists, theologians and business men. God has wrought wonderfully among us. God is still opening the way for greater progress. The cry is loud and long all along the line for consecrated workers. The harvest truly is white but the laborers are few.

"A last thing, we would urge upon you by way of application. We need more earnestness and simplicity in proclaiming the gospel. Our fathers were men of one book. They received power from on high by constant prayerfulness, and proclaimed earnestly and plainly what they understood. They felt like Paul, 'Though I preach the gospel, I have nothing to glory of; necessity is laid upon me; yea, woe is me if I preach not the gospel. The gospel is the intervention of Jesus Christ to save lost men. It is heaven's appointed remedy for man's malady; and the directions for taking the medicine must be so plain that the fool may take it assured of the fact that he will be healed. The gospel is a ship loaded with the bread of life, and must be brought so near the landing that the hungry can reach forth and take the bread of life. The gospel is the announcement of reconciliation between God and the sinner, a message of mercy, the history of the advent of Christ, His life, miracles, death, burial, resurrection, ascension and intercession. The gospel is the Messiah's conquering, triumphal car. There is power and magnetism about it. It is the power of God unto salvation to every one that believeth. It must be preached in its purity, in its simplicity, and with blood-earnestness. Man has been honored of God in being chosen to carry this holy message. Beginning a new century in the history of our denomination, let us carry this message with the same earnestness as did our fathers. Discourage inactivity, coldness, indifference, formalism in our preaching, and denounce spasmodic religion among our hearers. Contend earnestly for those principles which have been the very life of Baptists. The gospel must go, like the sun shining in his strength, scattering all clouds from the face of the world, until the moon and the stars shall be lost in its effulgence."

GO FORWARD.

The following extract is from a sermon preached by Dr. Walker before the Walker Baptist Association at Summerville, near Augusta, Ga., in September, 1899. Following the sermon, he raised a cash collection of $342.00 for the Walker Baptist Institute from poor country farmers.

"'And the Lord said unto Moses, Wherefore criest thou unto me? Speak unto the children of Israel, that they go forward.'—Exodus 14:15.

"For more than 400 years the Israelites had been slaves in Egypt. God's time for deliverance had come. Moses, his servant, is sent as ambassador to the court of Egypt with divine credentials to represent the court of heaven. Pharaoh refuses to obey the mandates of the mighty God, and ten or more plagues are sent upon the land. The cruel ruler decides to let Israel go. The mighty host, about three million strong, began their march. The pillar of cloud by day and the pillar of fire by night led them; they start out on the wilderness route, a distance of over four hundred miles. They rallied at Rameses, and marched out in wide columns.

"The Israelites were on foot. They were pursued by Pharaoh with 600 chosen chariots, and all the chariots of Egypt, and captains over each of them. The very flower of the Egyptian army hotly pursued the people of God; and, as Israel came to the Red Sea, at a point where it was probably ten miles wide, they saw mountains on either side, the sea in front of them, and the Egyptian army behind them. Many of the Israelites became faint-

DR. CHARLES T. WALKER AT THIRTY YEARS OF AGE.

hearted and murmured against Moses. He said unto them: 'Stand still, see the salvation of God, for the Egyptians you have seen to-day you will see no more forever.' Moses seemed to have been praying to God secretly, for there is no record of his public prayer. Yet the Lord said unto him, 'Wherefore criest thou unto me? Speak unto the children that they go forward.' Man's extremity is God's opportunity. The last of man is the first of God—God takes up where man leaves off. Prayer, diligence and effort go together. There is a time to pray, and then a time to act, to move. God seemed to say, 'You have prayed—now obey orders. Go forward.' The leaders moved off to the edge of the sea; the mighty waters divided—the Eternal God cut a pathway for the moving caravan. It was in the morning watch, or between 2 o'clock in the morning and sunrise. The king of day soon dispelled the darkness, and all day long the tramp, tramp of the footsteps of the Israelites was heard passing between the giant mountains of water. The angel, who had guarded them and led them, changed his position from front to rear, and got between the Israelites and the Egyptians. The Eternal God fully protects his people. As the last column of Israel passed, the Egyptian host came in. They traveled for a while as safely as did the Israelites, until the last chariot had left the bank, and when they were all out in the sea, and all Israel on the other side, Moses stretched out his rod over the sea, the waters came together and deluged the Egyptian army, while the Israelites saw the dead bodies of the Egyptians washed against the banks.

"I would have you notice that

"(1) Diligence and action must accompany prayer. Jesus taught his disciples to watch and pray. We are to pray for guidance, for direction, for strength, for conformity to God's will, for clean hearts, for the renewal of the Spirit, for the coming and extension of God's kingdom, and then watch and seize the opportunities for work under the guidance of the Holy Spirit. Joshua prayed, and then rallied his men while the sun stood still on Gibeon and the moon stood in the valley of Ajalon. God stopped the sun and moon; Israel did the fighting. A Quaker going along the Valley Forge road, heard some one in the thick brush praying. He turned aside to see who it was; he found a man in deep supplication, face suffused with tears, calling upon God for help. It was General Washington, praying for the success of the American army. He prayed for it, and then rose up and fought for it, and was victorious.

"(2) In order to go there must be reconciliation with God. The Lord is pledged to those who have become reconciled to him through Christ. Elijah built an altar, filled up the trenches, put the sacrifice upon the altar, got everything ready, and then prayed for fire. He was heard, for he was reconciled to God. Abraham was called from Mesopotamia to wander along the banks of the Euphrates; he left all he possessed for what was promised. He was reconciled to God. The language of the Christian is:

'My God is reconciled;
I hear his pardoning voice;
I can no longer fear;
With confidence I now draw near,
And Abba, Father, Abba, cry.'

"(3) They were not ordered to the right hand nor to the left, but to go forward. The road to victory is often through seas, through the fire, over mountains, through floods and through flames. We must go through the world's wild forest of tribulation, through the den of lions, over the mountains of leopards, through the fiery furnace, but we must go.

"(4) The guarding angel went from front to rear and stood between Israel and the Egyptian army—so did the cloud. They passed over and saw their enemies destroyed. When you obey God, he secures and protects you. The angels encamp around to deliver. Cæsar said to his boatmen: 'You can't sink, for you carry great Cæsar.' But the child of God can sing with boldness and assurance:

'How can I die while Jesus lives
As my Eternal God?
Who holds the earth's huge pillars up
And spreads the heavens abroad.

'How can I sink with such a prop
Who rose and left the dead?
Pardon and peace my soul receives
From my exalted head.' "

THE RESURRECTION.

The following is an extract from an Easter Sermon delivered by Dr. Walker at Mt. Olivet Baptist Church, April 7, 1901. The sermon was published in pamphlet form at the request of the church:

" 'To whom also he shewed himself alive after his passion by many infallible proofs, being seen of them forty days, and speaking of the things pertaining to the kingdom of God.'—Acts 1:3.

"The presence of the two angels in shining white from the glory world, and the empty grave were evidences of Christ's resurrection, but not infallible proofs. Technically speaking, they would be considered circumstantial evidence, but our text declares there were many infallible proofs of his resurrection.

"The infallible proofs of his resurrection are to be found in his appearances at different times in various places, to different people.

"First he appeared to Mary Magdalene. She recognized his voice, and said, 'Rabboni,' which means, 'My Master, my Teacher.' She recognized his loving voice and turned to grasp his hands, but he said, 'Touch me not, for I have not yet ascended to my God, and to your God; but tell Peter and my disciples I have gone before them into Galilee; there shall they see me.' Then he appeared to two disciples on the way to Emmaus, 7½ miles from Jerusalem, talking sadly, as they journeyed, on the crucifixion, and of their disappointment. Then Jesus, as he journeyed with them, began to speak of the fulfilment of the prophecy, and to rebuke them for their unbelief of the Scriptures; when their eyes became open, they found it was their Lord. The same evening he appeared to ten of them shut up in a room for fear of the Jews. Thomas being absent. Eight days after that time he appeared to eleven, Thomas being present. Paul states that he was seen of Peter. He met the disciples at the Sea of Tiberius. And then he was seen of the twelve, as he gave the marching order from Olivet's brow. He was seen of five hundred of the brethren at once. He was seen of James. Then Paul says, last of all, 'He was seen of me also, as of one born out of due time.'

"Christ's resurrection occurred at the time of year when nature was being revived from the effects of bleak winter; spring had burst forth in greenness and beauty, the birds were singing their cheerful lays—nature was vocal with His praise; earth was putting on her spring costume, representing a resurrection of all nature from the death and grave of the winter. So our Lord chose that season of the year to come out from the tomb when all nature was teaching the lesson of the resurrection.

"Christ's resurrection proved several things. It proved that he was the real Christ, the Holy One. They had said he was a deceiver. He had said that he would lay down his life and take it up again. Real divinity, which had never died, resurrected humanity. Here the Godhead sustained manhood and revived humanity. They killed his manhood, but divinity was untouched; and on the third day Divinity restored humanity to life.

"It settled the atonement, made it efficacious and gave power to the gospel If Christ had remained in the grave the claims of justice would have been unsatisfied; reconciliation between God and the sinner would not have been effected; heaven and earth could not have been united. Paul says: 'If Christ be not risen, our faith is vain; we are yet in our sins, and we are found false witnesses.' God sealed him as the world's Redeemer in his resurrection.

"It is a greater attestation of heaven's approval than the voice at his baptism, transfiguration, and prayer for special glorification. He proved his right to leadership. He dignified and exalted humanity. He reinstated man to favor with God. He founded his kingdom on the impregnable rock of truth, and the kingdoms of this world must become the kingdoms of our Lord and his Christ.

"His resurrection was necessary for our justification. For if he had not risen, man could not be justified with God, for our faith must rest upon a crucified, buried and risen Redeemer.

"His resurrection was necessary for the payment of the price of our redemption. It was to be a victory over sin, for he was to put away sin in the flesh and establish the reign of righteousness. It was to be a victory over the world; he was to have power in heaven and in earth, and hence must conquer the earth and subdue it; and his resurrection proved his power over nature, over disease, over death and over the grave.

"It was also a victory over Satan, for Satan was styled the prince of this world. The earth he claimed as his territory. He said to Jesus on the Mount of Temptation, that the world with all of its glory belonged to him, and he promised it to Christ if Christ would fall down and worship him. Christ chose to win the world by entering into conflict with Satan and overcoming him by his divine power.

"Ten years ago I stood on holy ground at the sepulchre where it is believed that our Lord was laid. And it seemed on that morning that I could hear again the message of the angels, 'He is not here, he is risen as he said; come, see the place where the Lord lay.' I bowed down on my knees and said, 'Thank God this is an empty tomb; the Lord is risen indeed.'

His resurrection was not only the stupendous manifestation of his power, but it was the exceeding greatness of his power. The Scripture gives us many exhibitions of the greatness of Christ's power. We have an exhibition of it in his first miracle, wrought at Cana of Galilee, when he turned the water into wine; there was a wonderful demonstration of power in stilling the tempest on the Sea of Galilee, when nature heard him and obeyed—the raging, surging billows calmed down at the voice of him who said, 'Peace, be still.' His giving sight to the blind, casting out devils, healing diseases, raising Lazarus, the widow's son of Nain, and the ruler's daughter, all were wonderful demonstrations of the power of the incarnate Christ. But the exceeding greatness of his power was not even seen in his causing darkness at high noon, while on Calvary, but it was the resurrecting of himself from the grave. O, thou living Christ, thou resurrected Jesus, live on to die no more! The exceeding greatness of thy power was seen in the resurrection of thyself from the dead!"

CHAPTER XVII.

EXTRACTS FROM ORATIONS AND ADDRESSES.

In this chapter will be found some extracts from orations and addresses delivered at different times and in different places by Dr. Walker. It has not been thought advisable to publish these addresses in full in this volume. For one thing, it would make the book too large for present purposes, and for another thing, it is proposed to issue later on a separate volume of his speeches and addresses, and also a volume of his sermons. These extracts will, nevertheless, serve to illustrate the lucid style of Dr. Walker and give some idea of the scope of the subjects treated by him from time to time.

Tuesday evening, Oct. 8, 1901, public memorial services were held in Mt. Olivet Baptist Church, New York City, by the Saloonmen's Protective Union No. 1, a benevolent association, in honor of the late President McKinley. Dr. Walker accepted the invitation to deliver the principal address. More than 2,000 people were present at the exercises. He delivered the following

EULOGY ON PRESIDENT MCKINLEY.

"It was said of Franklin when he died that the genius that had freed America and poured a flood of light over Europe had returned to the bosom of divinity. We are here this evening to honor the memory of our late President, who reunited the American nation, was the advance agent of protection and prosperity, universally beloved and deservedly popular. It is highly appropriate that the colored citizens of the metropolis of America should, in common with all other American citizens, pay honor to the noble-hearted, high-minded, Christian chief executive of the nation, who so recently passed to the great beyond.

"President McKinley came from the common people, and was always in sympathy with the masses. It was often said that he kept his ear close to the ground, listening for the voice of the people. It may be as truly said that he kept his ear open to hear the command of his Maker, for he had triumphant Christian faith.

* * * * * *

"Mr. McKinley came to the executive chair at a crucial period of the nation's existence. Hard times, strikes, unrest, scarcity of money, were problems with which he was confronted. The war with Spain was soon waged; grave problems had to be faced and solved, and all these he disposed of in a statesmanlike manner.

* * * * * *

"It has been claimed by many colored people that Mr. McKinley was not specially friendly to the Negro, and that colored men did not receive much recognition under his administration. Such a statement is made either because of ignorance of the truth or from misconception. I am one of those who believe the colored man should not stop to worry about position and office under any administration. That is a secondary consideration. Equal rights before the law, protection to life and property, the right to exist, the right to vote, the right to earn a living, the right to be a man, the right to be a *freedman* and a *freeman,* the right to expect equal and exact justice irrespective of creed, color or condition, is a greater privilege than being an officeholder. And yet, Mr. McKinley was the representative of a party which had enacted every piece of constructive legislation that we know anything about for the advancement of the colored people. Under his administration practical recognition was given to more colored citizens than under any other president. He appointed twelve men in the diplomatic and consular service. A colored man was appointed as Register of the Treasury, a colored man was appointed as Recorder of Deeds for the District of Columbia, a colored man was appointed United States Stamp Agent; colored men were appointed collectors of internal revenue in several States; collectors of ports, postmasters, collectors of census returns, land office registers, receivers of public moneys, and scores of minor Federal appointments throughout the country were given to colored men. Two distinguished colorel men were appointed paymasters in the U. S. V. during the Spanish-American War. In that same war, there were 260 colored commissioned officers and 15,000 enlisted men. In the 48th and 49th regiments, the President appointed 24 Negro captains, 50 Negro first lieutenants, 48 second lieutenants, with 2,688 enlisted men. It is estimated that, under Mr. McKinley's administration, colored men drew $8,477,000.

"Not only did the President show his interest in the race by these and other appointments, but by his visits to several of our Southern schools, such as Tuskegee, the Georgia State Industrial College, and the Prairie View Normal School in Texas. At each of these schools he made excellent speeches, in which he spoke handsomely of the military prowess and patriotism of 'the brave black boys,' as well as of the industrial and educational progress of the Negro.

*　　*　　*　　*　　*　　*

"There is uneasiness in some sections concerning the attitude of Mr. McKinley's successor toward our race. We have no cause to fear President Roosevelt. His past record entitles him to the confidence, love and respect of this American nation. He has a public record in times of peace and war of which this American nation should be proud. I have but to refer to him as Police Commissioner of New York City, as Assistant Secretary of the Navy, as Civil Service Commissioner, where he made it possible for a larger number of intelligent and worthy colored men to hold permanent positions than has been made possible by any other man in the nation. His administration as Governor of the Empire State was one of fairness and impartiality. He will always be remembered as leading the Rough Riders up San Juan Heights, through the high grass, cutting the barb-wire fences, repulsing the Spanish soldiers, capturing the block house, planting Old Glory on the ramparts of Santiago, hastening the surrender of General Toral to General Shafter, and thereby freeing oppressed, suffering, bleeding Cuba.

*　　*　　*　　*　　*　　*

"While Mr. McKinley made a great record as a soldier, statesman and president, he stands out conspicuously in the galaxy of presidents for his triumphant Christian faith. He said on one occasion, 'A religious spirit helps every man. It is at once a comfort and an inspiration, and makes one stronger, wiser and better in every relation of life. There is no substitute for it. It may be assailed by its enemies, as it has been, but they offer nothing in its place. It has stood the test of centuries, and has never failed to bless mankind.' He was shot by a ruthless assassin, Sept. 6, 1901. The conduct of the president at that tragic moment was like that of the Lord. In the shadow of death, as he had done in the executive mansion, he protested against mob violence, and said, referring to the murderer, 'Let no harm be done him.' Our dear dead President was again like our Christ when he said, just before yielding up the ghost, 'Good by; all, good bye; it is God's way; let his will be done, not ours.' His last prayer was one of submission and resignation to the will of the great God in whom he had so long trusted. And then, while standing on the interlacing margin of eternity, he repeated the Lord's prayer and chanted 'Nearer, my God, to thee, nearer to thee.' And lifting up his eyes on the land afar off, he beheld the King in his beauty, and fell on that long and tranquil sleep, hanging up his garments in the wardrobe of nations to rest until the archangel's trump shall disturb the long disordered creation, and soul and body shall be reunited.

* * * * * *

"The race of which we are members feels proud of the part played by James B. Parker in preventing the assassin from firing the third shot, though prejudice has prevented his receiving his due meed of praise. But let us not despair. Mr. McKinley is not dead to this American nation. He is still joined to us by the past, and by the still more glorious anticipations of the future. Heaven has discussed the sins of America as Lincoln, Garfield and McKinley, our martyred Presidents, have walked the golden streets, arm in arm. Too long have we winked at crime, lawlessness and anarchy. And we must yet learn that the highest citizen is not safe so long as the life of the lowest citizen is not protected."

From Dr. Walker's celebrated "Reply to Hannibal Thomas," which he has delivered in many American cities, next will be given two or three short extracts. The lecture, lengthened somewhat by additional facts and tables, has been published in pamphlet form. The pamphlet contains about 31 pages, and is well worth reading.

REPLY TO HANNIBAL THOMAS.

"Allow me to state that the author of 'The American Negro' has given us a book that will pass as a well-written, and in some respects, scholarly production. He has given important and interesting historical information and some advice that no sensible Negro will object to. On the other hand, he has made such sweeping charges against his own race — false charges, slanderous charges, malicious charges—as to entitle him to pass alongside of Judas Iscariot, Benedict Arnold and Aaron Burr, the trinity of traitors.

* * * * * *

"In his chapter on 'Characteristic Traits,' Mr. Thomas charges that the Negro represents an illiterate race, in which cowardice, ignorance and idleness are rife. In reply, I ask that Mr. Thomas read the history of the wars of this country from colonial times to the present days. Let him acquaint himself with the 54th Massachusetts regiment in the late Civil War; let him inform himself of the deportment of Negro soldiers at Cold Harbor, Fort Pillow, Fort Donelson, Fort Wagner, Port Royal, Port Hudson, Petersburg and Palmetto Ranch. Let him learn something about San Juan Hill and El Caney. Then ask him about this charge. It will fall of its own weight. As to ignorance among the colored race, it may be stated that they have decreased their illiteracy by nearly one-half since emancipation; they have given $13,000,000 towards their own education; they have 17,000 graduates; 500 doctors; 400 lawyers; 1,000 authors; 5 banks; 6 magazines, and 500 newspapers. At the close of the war, there were not more than 75 Negro teachers in the United States. To-day, we have more than 30,000 men and women of the race engaged in teaching school. There are yet many ignorant Negroes, just as there are still many ignorant whites, and the whites had a start on us of 250 years. As to idleness, there is a great deal of idleness among colored people—that is true; but you will find a smaller number of idlers, loafers, beggars and tramps among colored people in proportion to their numbers than among any other race. His criticism on Northern teachers who entered the South immediately after the war to lift up the recently emancipated Negro is unwarranted, as well as is the slap at Northern philanthropists for making contributions out of their princely munificence toward removing illiteracy among Southern Negroes. Their money was wisely spent, as can be clearly seen in the thousands of men and women who have been trained at these mission schools. The great men and women who went from the North to teach the despised Negro did the best work of their lives. Hampton Institute would have done good for the race if it had not educated any other man except Booker T. Washington; for he has inspired his entire race, and is to-day doing for the race what a thousand Hannibal Thomases could not do. Hannibal Thomas is pessimistic; Booker T. Washington is optimistic. Hannibal Thomas is grumbling; Booker Washington is working.

"With regard to Negro men seeking to marry white women, it is untrue of the masses. Nearly all of our men are satisfied to marry the women of the race to which they belong. We have women as good and as pure and as beautiful as any other race; and, as to variety, we excel them.

"I state it as my opinion that the solution of the so-called Negro Problem does not depend upon emigration, amalgamation nor colonization. The Negro must learn that character, industry, education and money are the essential prerequisites for intelligent citizenship. Let the American white man decide to lend a helping hand to his struggling black brother on life's highway; give him justice, equal and exact justice, North and South, East and West."

At the famous Golden Rule Meeting held at Calvary Baptist Church, West 57th Street, New York City, March 26, 1901, Dr. Walker represented the Negro race. The object of the Golden Rule Society is to do away with race prejudice and religious intolerance as far as possible. Jews, the followers of Confucius, and Protestants took part in the meeting. Rabbi Schulman and Rabbi Silverman represented the Jews, Wu Ting-fang, the Chinese minister to this country, represented Confucianism, and Dr. R. S. MacArthur, the pastor of Calvary Baptist Church, and one of the very ablest pulpit orators and lecturers in the world, Gen. T. L. James, Dr. R. Heber Newton, Edwin Markham, the poet, and Dr. Walker were among the prominent Protestants on the program. Dr. Walker was the only colored speaker and was next to the last on the list of participants. More than three thousand people were packed into Calvary's great auditorium. The audience had already been kept for nearly two hours when it came his

REV. CHARLES T. WALKER, ON HIS RETURN FROM HIS TRIP TO THE HOLY LAND, AGE THIRTY THREE YEARS.

time to speak, many hundreds having been compelled to stand during that long time. There was some interest, at least the interest of curiosity, to see and hear the colored man, and it was thought by a few that there was some misgiving on the part of the promoters of the meeting, because no one knew just what he would say or just what course he would take. An ill-timed word, an ill-considered expression on his part, might have cast a dampness over the meeting—might, in fact, have destroyed the very purpose for which the meeting was called. But he discussed his subject, "The Golden Rule as an Individual Motto," without one single mention of the Race Question in an offensive and undignified way. He made his mark, and won a great place for Negro leaders on that memorable night. Of the ten or twelve speeches made that night, the metropolitan press the next morning united in saying that the honors of the evening were carried off by Mr. Wu Ting-fang and Dr. Walker. As Wu Ting-fang was the honored guest of the occasion, it seemed courteous to couple his name with that of the man who made the best speech of the evening and won the greatest applause. Dr. Walker caught the crowd at the outset by announcing that if any one doubted the sincerity of the promoters of the Golden Rule Meeting, their doubts would be dispelled so soon as they saw him on the platform to make an address; for, said he, so far as he knew, his race identity had never been questioned. This sally provoked great laughter and applause, because Mr. Walker is a very dark-skinned Negro, and the audience saw at once the wit and humor of his statement and appreciated it.

THE GOLDEN RULE AS AN INDIVIDUAL MOTTO.

"All men are the workmanship of the same Almighty Father. God made of one blood all nations to dwell on the face of the earth. All are alike subjected to sin and infirmity; all are responsible beings, and all alike are hastening to an eternity of righteous retribution. All men are members of the same social family. No man, therefore, can injure his fellowman without injuring himself. We build up ourselves and increase our happiness in proportion as we labor for the welfare of others. With the Golden Rule as an individual motto, will come the recognition of the Fatherhood of God and the universal brotherhood of man; and when this doctrine of the unity of the human family shall be believed and accepted by each individual, then man's inhumanity to man will cease; there will no longer be that monstrous indifference, when the question is asked, 'Where is Abel thy brother?' that replies, 'Am I my brother's keeper?' Yes, we are our brother's keeper, and this motto will not only connect man with his Creator, but will also connect man with man.

"This motto will include justice and fair play. Many of the courts of our land known as temples of justice are misnamed; they are but temples of injustice. Justice should hold an even balance. Justice should make no inquiry as to racial identity. Justice should have no kin people. With this motto adopted by every individual, each man will have an equal chance in the race of life; equal and exact justice will be given to all; a healthy public sentiment will be created in favor of law and order; law itself is weak and helpless unless upheld and supported by public sentiment.

"We should adopt the Golden Rule as an individual motto, for it will produce an era of peace and good-will among men; it will become the prophetic music of the ages. The Golden Rule will cause us to see humanity not only as it is, but humanity as it shall be. Not Lazarus, the beggar at the rich man's gate, full of sores —a mass of corruption and putrifying sores; but Lazarus in Abraham's bosom; humanity redeemed; humanity regenerated, reorganized, reanimated, reconstructed and relighted with heavenly glory. This motto will prepare us for the grand reunion of the human family in the last day. The sons of Noah who separated in the Plain of Shinar will one day hold a reunion. I believe in the theory of the unity of the human family, and that it is the order of divine Providence that these long separated brethren must meet again. Shem went into Asia, Japhet into Europe, and Ham into Africa. At the reunion, Shem will be represented in the person of the despised Chinaman and Japanese; Japhet in the person of the proud and cultured Caucasian, and Ham in the person of the despised, rejected and oppressed Negro. And I promise you that the sons of Ham will make a creditable showing when the reunion takes place."

At Carnegie Hall, New York City, on Sunday evening, May 27th, 1900, Dr. Walker shook the country by an able and patriotic address on the so-called Race Question. The hall was packed from pit to dome by an audience of fully 8,000 souls, white and black. The speech, which he called "An Appeal to Cæsar," was a review of the Conference on the Race Question held a short time before that at Montgomery, Ala., and in which such men as Bourke Cochran, John Temple Graves, Dr. H. B. Frissell, Governor MacCorkel and others participated, and was also a reply to some strictures heaped upon the race in Carnegie Lyceum the Sunday before by A. Rev. Henry Frank. The newspapers in the metropolis and throughout the country published extracts from Dr. Walker's address, and the speech won the orator much fame, as well as the title, "the defender of his race." Following are extracts from

AN APPEAL TO CAESAR.

"It is my desire to speak to you on this occasion concerning a race of people greatly misrepresented, despised, oppressed and hated; a race peculiarly situated and everywhere spoken against. I appear in behalf of a people born in tribulation and disciplined in the hard school of slavery; opposed and persecuted, as it has been, by some of the brightest minds that ever spoke or wielded a pen, and yet defended by some of the ablest, purest and noblest men and women the earth has ever known; among the latter may be mentioned Charles Sumner, Horace Greeley, William Lloyd Garrison, Wendell Phillips, Henry Ward Beecher, Mrs. Harriet Beecher Stowe, Dr. Nathan Bishop, Mrs. Benedict and a host of others.

"From this great hall on last Sunday the news went out to the world that one Henry Frank, in preaching the gospel of the Lowly Nazarene, stated in the prelude to his discourse that the Negro should again be reduced to the slavery of ante-bellum days.

* * * * * *

"I have now given you a hasty survey of Mr. Frank's utterances and also some of the unfavorable criticisms of the gentlemen who were among the participants at the recent Montgomery Conference. Now let me give you the colored man's side. First, the Negro is an American citizen; he is a member of the body politic; he has been in this country almost as long as anybody else. The amendment to the constitution did not make us men. God made us men before man made us citizens. The amendment was only a recognition of the God-given rights of the colored man. Second, the emancipation of the colored race was the overruling providence of God. Slavery was wrong, and the time had come in the Providence of the mighty God that the battalions of the righteous army of God should march against the giant walls of slavery, and slavery fell like Dagon before the ark. Although Mr. Lincoln wrote the immortal proclamation liberating 4,000,000 human beings, which was the central act of his administration and the most glorious event of the nineteenth century, yet the hand that wrote the proclamation was guided by the bruised and pierced hand of the incarnate Christ. The 15th amendment to the Constitution of the United States, under which the colored man acquired the right to vote, was placed there after the nation had been baptized in blood, and it will require a second baptism of blood to remove it. Third, the colored man's right to citizenship cannot be denied on any ground—human or divine. Citizenship is due the Negro as a reward for his meritorious service on the battlefield. As early as 1770, Crispus Attucks, during the Boston massacre, led in the bloody drama which opened up a new and thrilling chapter in American history. He attacked the main guard of the ministerial army and went down in his own blood before the terrible fire, the first man to give his life for American independence. He is known in history as a soldier, patriot and martyr. And from that day down to the records of yesterday, the Negro has fought, bled and died for this country, and his bones have been left to bleach on a thousand battlefields. What has the Negro done to be maligned, maliciously assailed and inhumanly persecuted as he is?

* * * * * *

"The Negro only asks for simple justice—that is all. He would have an equal chance in the race of life. He wants better opportunities. He wants to be admitted to the industrial and mechanical trades. He wants a chance to earn a living. He is striving to be honest, industrious, intelligent, economical and self-reliant. He wants his manhood recognized and encouraged rather than choked and stifled. He wants his white brother to dethrone prejudice and enthrone reason; remove hatred and place love in its stead."

The following extract is from a lecture by Dr. Walker delivered in many cities during the past year. The subject of the lecture was:

THE COLORED MEN FOR THE TWENTIETH CENTURY.

"True education is the development of power; its mission is to prepare men and women for the duties of life. There should be round, full, symmetrical development. A cultured brain and a corrupt heart frequently produces a demon, while a good heart without an enlightened brain may produce a sentimentalist. That education which isolates and walls off from the masses is a curse. We are blessed to be a blessing; nature receives to impart.

"We must be mechanics, skilled in industrial arts, a noble band of professional men, of business men. Men must prepare for the pulpit. We demand skill and ability in our professional men, and our churches must demand moral and intellectual strength on the part of those who fill the pulpit. An ignorant man in the pulpit is more dangerous than a quack doctor in a family. The man who preaches the gospel deals with immortal souls, and it is highly important that he be 'a workman that needeth not to be ashamed, rightly dividing the word of truth.'

"I do not believe in special education for the colored man. He needs the same kind of education as other people. He has proven his susceptibility to the highest intellectual attainment, and, while he needs industrial training, he should strive to secure the highest possible development along all lines. Every mind was made for growth and development and its nature is sinned against when it is doomed to ignorance. It is better to have a dead body hung to one than a dead mind.

"Our spiritual development must be commensurate with our intellectual advancement. There will be a series of conflicts between wickedness and righteousness, between virtue and vice, between truth and error; if we would join the crusade of virtue against vice, the army of righteousness against wickedness, there must be spiritual progress.

"The colored man is a bona fide American citizen; he is no Afro-American; he is a full-fledged American citizen; this country is his home, and the American flag is his flag. He is a part of the history of this great nation; a part of the body politic—bone of her bone, flesh of her flesh—her near kinsman, the brother of Shem and Japheth. Our forefathers felled the timbers, cleared the forests, bedewed the soil with their sweat, tears and blood, built up the country and perpetuated its history. They fought in all the wars from the Revolutionary struggle until this time, and even now are represented in the Philippines by our brave soldier boys. It is high time that we were claiming this as our home. Most that has been said and written concerning emigration has been written by foreigners who came to this country to find a home, and now, guilty of base ingratitude, they are talking of emigration or colonization for others.

"The twentieth century will demand that class of young men who will support the dignity of their nature. Men who will use aright their powers and capacities; men who will respect the women of their race, who will feel proud of them and their accomplishments.

"The new century is coming laden with treasuries, new gifts of heaven, hopes, aspirations, golden purposes, rings and bracelets for the adornment of personal character. The twentieth century is coming with new trials, new joys, new opportunities and increased responsibilities. The new century is coming as the bearer of glad tidings, ambassador of peace—herald of the great king.

"Let the men of the twentieth century arise, prepare to face the problems of life, to play the men for their people and for the cities of our God.

'We live in deeds, not years; in thoughts, not breaths;
In feelings, no figures on a dial;
We should count time by heart throbs. He most lives
Who thinks most, feels noblest, acts the best.'"

CHAPTER XVIII.

EXTRACTS FROM NEWSPAPERS.

Following extracts from various newspapers will indicate how extensive Dr. Walker's work has been, and how highly it has been appreciated by the people, white and black, North and South:

From the Examiner, New York City's Baptist newspaper, Feb. 22nd, 1900:

"President A. B. Sears was in the chair at the meeting of the City Ministers' Conference. Rev. C. N. Mitchell, of Toronto, who was on his way to his new mission field in Bolivia, and Rev. James T. McGovern, who has been preaching at the Emmanuel Church, and was recently appointed missionary to Spain, were introduced. Mr. W. Henry Grant, Assistant General Secretary of the Ecumenical Conference on Foreign Missions, presented the financial needs of the Conference, and spoke of the great good which will result in missionary stimulus from the meetings to be held in Carnegie Hall, April 21 to May 1. The paper of the morning was presented by Rev. Dr. Charles T. Walker, Pastor of the Mount Olivet Church. He discussed his topic, "Truth from Another Angle on the Negro Problem," with so much freshness and power that the conference requested it for publication and voted money to cover the cost. The distinguishing feature of the paper was the fact that Dr. Walker ascribed the prejudice against the Negro race to racial rather than sectional antipathies. He gave an outline of Negro advancement along religious, educational and financial lines, pleaded for simple justice for the Negro, and urged that all avenues of progress should be open to him on the simple qualification of manhood and character."

From the New York Sun, Nov. 1899:

"The Mt. Olivet Baptist Church, African, which was but a few months ago torn by the dissensions between the Rev. Daniel W. Wisher, who was then its pastor, and the majority of his congregation, demonstrated yesterday that its troubles have not affected the vigor of the church, but have rather awakened it to new strength. Since the new pastor, the Rev. Dr. Charles T. Walker, was installed there have been revival meetings seven nights a week, and new converts have been made to the number of 110. Of these, the seventy-six who seemed to the pastor and deacons most worthy were baptized at the morning service yesterday.

"The news of so great a baptism had spread about among other Baptist congregations among the colored people of the city, and had been almost enviously commented upon in Methodist circles. At half past ten o'clock yesterday morning half an hour before the service was to begin, every seat was filled and the tact of the ushers had to be exercised to the utmost to dispose properly of the streams of people that came pouring down to the big gray church from the east and west under the shadow of the elevated railroad tracks. At a quarter before 10 o'clock the outside doors of the church were locked and after that only those who were related to the candidates to be baptized were admitted. The candidates themselves had taken the precaution to come very early. For an hour after the church doors were closed a constantly increasing crowd of the disappointed stood on the steps and on the sidewalk and bewailed their lack of foresight in not coming earlier.

"The volume of sound with which the great congregation rolled out the full strains of the opening hymn, 'Blow, ye, the trumpet blow,' was enough to have raised a less emotional congregation to a high state of religious exaltation. It was some time after the 'Amen' that closed the song before the undertone of joyful exultation quite subsided. The Rev. Dr. Walker preached on 'Christ, the Living Rock.' His text was: 'And did all drink the same spiritual drink; for they drank of that spiritual Rock that followed them: and that Rock was Christ.'

"Fifty women were immersed in just twenty-five minutes. It took twenty-six minutes to baptize the twenty-six men. After the closing hymn, 'Rock of Ages,' had been sung in a mighty chorus that made the great church seem to sway with the harmony, the Rev. Dr. Walker, with his wet garments still upon him, dismissed the congregation with a prayer. Few left the church until they had congratulated the newly-baptized members most heartily."

From the New York World, March 12, 1900:

"What is believed to be the largest number of persons ever baptized at one time within a building were submerged yesterday morning at the Mt. Olivet Baptist Church, on Fifty-third Street near Seventh Avenue, by the Rev. C. T. Walker, who is known among those of his race as the 'Black John the Baptist.'

"Five weeks ago a revival was begun. As a result the membership of the church has increased 483. Two hundred and thirty-four of the new members had never been baptized. Yesterday it was arranged that 184 of them should be submerged.

"Long before 11 o'clock, the hour set for the opening of the services, the big church was packed to its utmost capacity, and those who could not get inside the doors were lined along Fifty-third Street. At 10:30 o'clock the street was completely blocked, and a squad of policemen from the West Forty-seventh Street Station had to be called to clear the way.

"The pool, which is of marble, is in the rear of the rostrum, with steps leading to it from either side. The water was between three and four feet deep. The Rev. Mr. Walker and Deacon G. H. Webb stood in the centre of it. Three men stood on the steps on each side to assist the candidates.

"The first person to be led up was Octavia Adams, who had been cook in the family of Robert Ingersoll for ten years. While on the steps of the pool she said that as long as she had known Col. Ingersoll she had been a firm believer in all of his doctrines, but she now realized the power and the goodness of God. She was full of enthusiasm, and after she had been taken out and dressed, she went back to the church and encouraged those who were to follow her.

"First of the men to be led up was the old blind man who is such a familiar sight at the Fifty-ninth Street Park entrance. He is nearly eighty years old and had to be carried to the edge of the pool.

"The congregation was greatly excited. Women in all parts of the church tore their hats from their heads and shouted wildly. During the last half hour of the service six of them fainted."

From the New York Journal, March 12, 1900.

"Yesterday was a day of jubilee and joy in the Mt. Olivet Baptist Church. The fruits of the five weeks of the soul-stirring revival were gathered. Converts to the number of 184 men, women children, boys and girls, were baptized by immersion amid such scenes of praises as are not likely to be forgotten by the hundreds present. To take the figures of the happy elders, it was a record breaking event in New York for 408 recent converts to gather in fellowship in a meeting last night; this result was especially gratifying because of the recent dissensions in Mt. Olivet Church. For a time there was the trouble and then came a rallying cry and with it a new leader—the Rev. C. T. Walker, of the Tabernacle Baptist Church of Augusta, a preacher of forcible ability and intense religious zeal, sometimes called the colored 'John the Baptist.' Under the pastorate of Mr. Walker, Mt. Olivet has thrived. The baptismal services yesterday morning attracted a tremendous congregation. Long before the doors opened the crowd was pressing at the doors of the pretty church, 53rd Street and Broadway. The morning sermon was preached by Rev. Silas X. Floyd, the successor of Mr. Walker in Augusta. The subject was, 'Pleasing God."

"The baptismal services followed. The marble baptismal tank sunk in the pulpit platform was opened. The candidates for baptism, 144 women in white flannel baptismal robes, and 40 men in black, met in the Sunday school rooms in the basement which was divided into two sections.

"For three hours, Mr. Walker and his assistant, Deacon Webb, stood waist deep in the tnk and conducted the baptismal services.

"The religious enthusiasm of the congregation was intense. Three women and two men fainted after leaving the tank. Converts and members became hoarse, with their cries for blessing and approval; an hysterical cry from a newly baptized convert dripping with water on leaving the tank was followed by choruses of glad cries. The baptism of a little blind girl was followed by a tumult of enthusiasm.

" 'Indeed, this reminds me of a day in the old South,' said Mr. Floyd, his eyes glowing with religious emotion.

"With but brief intervals, hymns were sung with striking fervor. A brother who sat on the platform led a series of old-fashioned, Southern camp-meeting hymns. One was:

I have a little book I carry with me,
It tells me all about heaven and Galilee,
  By and bye.
When the storm of life is over,
We'll anchor in the harbor,
We will praise God forever,
  Bye and bye.'

"Such hymns were sung with the intonation peculiar to the singing of colored congregations in the South. Men and women arose, and as the singing progressed, their bodies rocked and their feel kept time to the swing of the melodies.

"The greatest single victory over sin in the minds of those present was the conversion and baptism of Mrs. Octavia Adams, of No. 117 E. 21st St., the city home of the late Col. Robert G. Ingersoll. Mrs. Adams had been a cook in the family for years."

From New York Tribune, March 12, 1900:

"One hundred and eighty-four persons were baptized by immersion at Mt. Olivet Baptist Church, Fifty Third Street, near

Broadway yesterday morning. Of this number 89 were women. In all 408 persons were received into the church. It was originally intended that 233 persons should be received in the church by baptism, but of that number 49 did not present themselves. The remainder were received into the church on profession of faith. The baptismal ceremonies were conducted by Rev. C. T. Walker, the pastor of the church, and Deacon Webb.

"During the baptism ceremonies religious fervor was worked up to such a state that several women and two men fainted. Three women fainted while being immersed. All, however, were revived.

"For five weeks, the Rev. Mr. Walker has been conducting revival services in the church, and yesterday's ceremonies were the result of the work of conversion.

"Anticipating the crush that would be at the church, and fearful that there might be trouble in handling it, Capt. Donohue, of the West 47th Street Station, detailed five patrolmen from his command to remain at the church during the services. Several times the patrolmen were forced to resort to rather rough tactics in order to keep the big crowd in check. Finally at the request of the church officials, the police cleared the big corridors of the church and drove several hundred persons who were late in arriving into the street.

"The jam about the church was terrific. Every conceivable vantage point was taken inside the big auditorium long before the services were begun.

"People were jammed in the church like sardines. They filled the aisles and stood about three or four deep about the pulpit. Some time before the service began, the church was filled and the police were instructed not to allow more to enter. Then began a wild scramble. In a few minutes there were fully 1,000 persons struggling in the vestibule and on the pavement outside the church.

"The candidates for baptism were seated in the center of the church, the women on one side of the aisles, while the men, black-robed and in their stocking feet, were on the other side.

"The women were all clad in loose fitting white flannel gowns. The majority of them had white ribbons in their hair. The regular sermon was preached by Rev. S. X. Floyd of Augusta, Ga.

"The women were baptized first, the children and men last. The first to be immersed was a little blind girl; as she was brought up dripping from the big tank she cried, 'Thank God, I am saved.' The child's cry was taken up by the big congregation.

"While the men were being baptized somebody in the congregation began singing, 'Bye-and-bye'; the song was quickly taken up by the entire congregation and the religious enthusiasm was increased. Men and women arose in their seats, and while they sang they waved books and handkerchiefs.

"It was announced by the Rev. Mr. Walker that on the list of converts were men and women from every clime. There were several blind, deaf and dumb. Mr. Walker said that among those who received baptism was a colored woman who for many years had been employed in the household of the late Robert G. Ingersoll, the agnostic."

From the New York Times, May 7, 1900:

"Mount Olivet Baptist Church celebrated yesterday its 22nd anniversary with afternoon and evening meetings. The exercises were held in Carnegie Hall which was crowded not only with the members of the congregation, but with colored Odd Fellows and other societies and colored residents of the different boroughs.

"The meeting was more or less a congratulatory one to the Rev. Dr. C. T. Walker, whose pastorate began seven months ago, when he came here from Augusta Ga. The Trustees' report showed that the church had had the most prosperous year in its existence, and although covert references were made by the speakers to the troubles of the Rev. Mr. Wisher, the old sores have been healed and everybody was in harmony.

"In April of last year the church was in debt exclusive of a mortgage of $19,500, in the sum of $1,400 with $100.80 in the treasury. Since then there have been paid for running expenses $6,168.88, and there is now a balance on hand of $899.71. Within Dr. Walker's pastorate, over 800 members have been added.

"The collection yesterday morning brought in $1,269.16. At the evening services this sum was swelled to $1,634.46. To this will be added $1,000 taken in at recent collections. The announcement was made that John D. and William Rockefeller were among the contributors in the past and that the City Mission had borne the 'white man's burden' in helping to raise the big church debt to the amount of $9,000.

"The Rev. Dr. R. S. MacArthur, of Calvary Baptist Church, spoke in complimentary terms of the work of Dr. Walker.

" 'I consider him the most valuable acquisition to the ministry of this great city,' he said. 'If you can spare him for some service I want him to come and speak in Calvary. My people want good preaching, and he is a good preacher. And if you will put up with me, I'll come to you for one service.' (Laughter and applause followed this remark.)

"Dr. MacArthur then made a plea for general education among the colored people, and said: 'It has made me boil with indignation when I have seen the door shut in the face of black men and opened to white men with black hearts.'"

From the Augusta (Ga.) Chronicle, March 20, 1900:

"Rev. C. T. Walker, the 'Black Spurgeon,' who has lately acquired the sub-name of the 'Black John the Baptist' by the big results of the recently held revival in New York, delivered a strong lecture at his former church, Tabernacle Baptist, on Ellis Street, last night to a crowded house.

"The subject used by Rev. Walker was 'The Negro for the Twentieth Century.' He took as a special theme the necessity of the Negro race patronizing their own enterprises and learning to have confidence in themselves that the white race has in itself. He bore heavily upon the importance to his race of an industrial education.

"He said that the Negro must put aside the ante-bellum belief of their absolute dependence upon the whites and stand solely upon their own efforts. He said that prejudice was very general against the colored man and it rested entirely with him whether in the days to come the race will attain that place which it should attain. He especially advised his hearers to spread the necessity of character-building among their people that this end might be reached. They should all think more of upholding themselves individually and collectively; they must all have more respect for their women, since in them, to a great degree, lives what the leaders of the race are working for. The parents should be especially particular to see that their boys and girls were educated in the trades, that they may be taught the hurtfulness of idleness and the profit of being always employed at something which would be beneficial.

"At the conclusion of his address, to make this point more forceful, he asked all of the professional and business men present to stand up. A large number responded, and he pointed them out as an example for the idle to follow."

From the Fall River, Mass., Evening News:

"The people who turned out to hear Rev. C. T. Walker, D. D., speak at the Royal Arcanum Hall, on Bank Street, on Thursday night, were abundantly rewarded for ignoring the rain. Dr. Walker is one of the best known colored men in this country. He ranks with Booker T. Washington in prominence, and has won this prominence through intelligence and ability. He is now Pastor of Mount Olivet Baptist Church in New York City, one of the largest and strongest churches among the colored people of the North. His reputation as a more than local man of note was won while he was pastor of the Tabernacle Baptist Church of Augusta, Ga. He secured the funds to erect the building, and made the church one of the biggest among his people in the South.

"Dr. Walker is a remarkable man, one whom it would repay anybody to meet. He was born a slave in 1858. Left an orphan when only eight years of age, he worked as a field hand until he was fifteen years old, when he began to study for the ministry. Largely through his own efforts he has become a man of notably large and broad education. He has traveled extensively, and has a great fund of material for use both in the pulpit and in talks and lectures. When one has heard him talk the main element of his notable success in life becomes apparent. He is a born orator. His gift has been cultivated to fine advantage. He has that quality of voice which makes speaking to large assemblies of people no difficult task. There is no suggestion of the shouting preacher in his method, but his voice carries naturally and easily. It was apparent that he was accustomed to speaking in much larger halls than the one in which he was heard last night. His voice was rather crowded there when he was specially earnest. He is very eloquent and may well be called 'The Black Spurgeon of America.' His fund of humor is inexhastible. This humor took well with his audience. Many of those present were old acquaintances."

From the Georgia Baptist (Augusta, Ga.), July 20, 1899.

"It has been known for some weeks that the Mount Olivet Baptist Church, of New York City, with fifteen hundred present, had extended a unanimous call to Dr. C. T. Walker, of our city, to accept its pastorate.

"The universal hope of our community has been that Dr. Walker would decline this call as flattering as it is and remain in Augusta. No man in Augusta has a deeper hold upon the whole community than Dr. Walker. His success as a pastor of Tabernacle Baptist Church in this city for the past fourteen years has been phenomenal and humanly speaking it does not appear that a man can be found to take his place at this church. Aside from Tabernacle Church, all the people of Augusta, white and colored, are anxious that Dr. Walker remain in Augusta. Should he decide to accept the call to New York, Dr. Walker will leave behind him thousands of loving hearts whose prayers will follow him wherever his lot may be cast."

From the Augusta (Ga.), Chronicle, March 27, 1901:

"Will D. Upshaw, of Mercer University, who spent Sunday

and part of yesterday in Augusta, left for Macon at 4 o'clock yesterday afternoon. He is re urning from a stay of several months in New York, where he has been in the interest of a loan fund at Mercer, and where, as press reports and his subscription list indicate, he did some excellent and successful work for the great Georgia College.

"Speaking of preachers in New York, Mr. Upshaw said, 'Many people in Augusta will be gratified to learn that your city recently sent to the metropolis a man who is preaching to the largest crowds of any man in New York, either white or colored. I refer to none other than Charles T. Walker, 'The Black Spurgeon,' so long and favorably known in Augusta. I confess that as a Georgian, I felt a great deal of pride and congratulation for my own State, to see with my own eyes the remarkable work he is doing and hear on all sides many expressions of commendation concerning him. I had the pleasure of speaking in his church several times. On the Sunday night on which I spoke, 1,500 people packed the house, and on another occasion, in company with Dr. Frank Rogers Morse, the accomplished associate pastor of Calvary Church, I attended the services and heard the pastor preach to an overflowing audience that crowded floor and galleries, and it is no disparagement to the white brethren to say that his sermon was one of the most forceful I heard in the metropolis. Dr. Walker's congregations are growing until he has to hold overflow meetings in the lecture room. You will find many Negroes of fine education and genuine culture while there is a refreshing sprinkling—I use the word 'refreshing' advisedly—of the old-fashioned 'Georgia darkey,' whom Alex Bealer describes so strikingly, who keeps the speaker in good spirits by the occasional lusty 'Amen.'

"When Dr. Walker took hold of the church, it had been somewhat divided by the political sermons of his predecessor; but the present pastor has had the good sense to steer clear of such breakers. Now the large church is united and harmonious, and much genuine good is being done. Dr. Morse, who often acts as an advisory friend of the colored church, in speaking to me of the new pastor, said, 'Mr. Walker is a true man, really a remarkable man, and the work he is doing is marvelous.'

"In speaking of the contribution which Rev. Charles T. Walker is making to the solution of the race problem by his presence and work in the North, Mr. Upshaw said:

"'I have heard Rev. Walker deliver an address by special request of the New York Baptist ministers' conference, which, while true to his race, as all honest men wanted him to be, was so fair and sensible that he deserves the commendation of all white men, and especially all Southern men. In that Northern atmosphere, where many of his hearers not only expected but possibly wished this distinguished Southern Negro to flay his former neighbors, Charlie Walker had the common sense not to make one single sectional allusion. He never used the words "North" or "South," throughout his entire address. He discussed the sad fact of undue race prejudice, not from a sectional but a racial standpoint, and plead with an eloquence that was as touching as it was thrilling, that his race be admitted to progress everywhere on the credentials of worth and justice.

"'Dr. C. O. Pope, so well known in Augusta, and now President of Simmons' College, in Texas, was in the audience, and when Dr. Walker sat down amid many cheers, and maybe, some tears, Dr. Pope arose and told the people that he was raised in the community with Charles Walker's father, and having known from boyhood the man who had addressed them, he wished to bear testimony to the worth of the man, and the truth and fairness of what he had said.

"'It was my own pleasure to supplement Dr. Pope's words along the same line and by an emphasis of what I had told the ministers' conference in a speech before Dr. Walker's coming—that if there were more Charles T. Walkers and Booker T. Washingtons, there would be less race problems in the South.'

"When the Chronicle reporter smiled and suggested that he was giving the former Augusta pas or very high praise, Mr. Upshaw smiled pleasantly in turn and said:

"'Yes, I know I am, but I am doing it deliberately and unreservedly.'

"'I believe that when a worthy Negro like Charles T. Walker, with faith in God and love for man, a humanity that cannot be spoiled by praise, breaks through conditions and tendencies that keep so many of his race below honor and progress, it is only just and right that his more fortunate white neighbor should give him the credit due, take him by the hand and say: "God bless you. If you are honestly trying to lift up yourself and your people, I will honestly help you to be true to yourself, to your people and to God."

From the Georgia Baptist, Nov. 15, 1901:

"No man, white or colored, has gone from the South to New York, the great commercial metropolis of this country, and made for himself in so short a time a reputation and friends that our Dr. Walker has.

"As highly regarded as he has been for years in Augusta, his real worth to the denomination, the country and the race has not been fully understood until he entered the pastorate in New York City. Mt. Olivet Baptist Church, of which he is pastor in New York, is no more anxious that he continue his labors with them than are the thousands of his friends outside of his church. The mass meeting, called at Mt. Olivet Church, Nov. 6, at which hundreds gathered to give expression to the great desire that Dr. Walker continue his work in that city, was presided over by the distinguished Dr. MacArthur, one of the leading white ministers of the country. Bishop W. B. Derrick led the speakers in eulogizing the work of Dr. Walker, and urging him to withdraw his resignation tendered to Mt. Olivet Church. The speakers on the program were men of note of all denominations and leading politicians who, as a rule, take no interest in religion.

"Dr. Walker's friends in Augusta, white and colored, can but feel gratified at his success in the North and the high regard which he has won from all classes. The Baptists of Georgia are ardently attached to Dr. Walker, and if he decides to return to his old charge, they will receive him back with open arms."

Testimonials similar to the above could be multiplied by the score. North, South, East and West, Dr. Walker is a man well spoken of by white and black, publican and sinner.

CHAPTER XIX.

ANECDOTES.

It is one of the unwritten laws of American civilization that the public has a right to get off jokes on leading public servants, whether they are clergymen, statesmen, business men or what not. Very often this habit of caricaturing our ablest men by cartoons and jokes is carried to extremes; but within proper limits, if it is possible to define what is proper in such a matter, there seems to be no objection to it among those who may be the victims. It is true that sometimes a joke, if founded on facts, will go further in illustrating a man's real disposition than perhaps anything else. At any rate, it is customary to include in every biography a chapter giving the anecdotal side of the subject's life. That rule will not be departed from in this case.

"THE BLACK STURGEON."

On one occasion Dr. Walker was preaching before the Walker Baptist Association down in Georgia. In the middle of his discourse, and at the close of one of his most thrilling flights of eloquence, an old colored man, in a frenzy of excitement, rose to his feet and exclaimed: "My Gawd! No wonder dey call him de Black Sturgeon!"

The old man evidently had mistaken the word "Spurgeon" for the word "Sturgeon." In speaking of the matter afterwards, Dr.

Walker said, with a good-natured laugh, "Well, I'm glad he did not class me with the small fish."

READING AND COUNTING FOR NEGROES.

Once a Georgia Negro carried a letter to Dr. Walker and asked him to read it for him. Dr. Walker complied with his request. Two or three days later, the same man came back and said:

"Doc, you sho did read my letter all right. I took it to two white men since, and dey read the same things dat you did."

Somewhat later, another colored man came to Dr. Walker and asked him how much was 9 x 70. Dr. Walker told him 630. A few days later the colored man returned and said:

"Doc, you know de uddah day, I axt you how much was 9 x 70, an' you told me 630. Well, I axt Capt. Jones (a white man) about it and he told me de same thing. I tell you, Doc, you sho knows how to count."

In telling these stories, Dr. Walker always makes the point that it is very difficult to get the average Negro to believe another Negro unless some white man will endorse what the colored man says. It seems to be an old and foolish way Negroes were taught during slavery.

PRAYING FOR MONEY.

Dr. Walker believes in praying for everything. In 1886, when in Boston trying to raise money to assist him with his church work at Augusta, he was rooming with Mr. Charles A. Dryscoll, who was at that time a student in the New England Conservatory of Music. One Saturday night Mr. Dryscoll noticed that several times during the night Dr. Walker got out of the bed. He asked him if he was sick. Dr. Walker replied, "No." Once, while Mr. Dryscoll watched to see what called him from the bed so often, he found him kneeling by a chair in prayer. He spent nearly the whole night in prayer. The next morning (Sunday morning) he went to the First Baptist Church, of which Dr. P. S. Moxom was then pastor, and made an appeal to the congregation for help. He secured $109.00 in cash and many pledges. Dr. Walker always referred to that contribution as prayer money.

PRAYING FOR CONVERTS.

Once at Augusta he commenced his revival services by making a request of the people that they would pray that the Lord would give them 200 converts during the meeting. At the close of six weeks' work the number of converts was found to be 325. But in a short while a large number of these converts proved such miserable failures as Christians, Dr. Walker said, if God would forgive him, he never would pray again for 200 converts, and he said that he did not want anybody else to pray that prayer in Tabernacle Church. He thought that the best thing to do was to pray for souls, and leave the number with God.

ABOUT JAY BIRDS.

Dr. Walker relates with great pleasure that, when he was a boy, he made it his business to kill every jay bird he saw. He said that the old folks had told him that he would never see any jay birds around on Fridays, because on Fridays all the jay birds went to carry sand to hell. So he made up his mind to kill every one he could, in order that the number of jay birds engaged in the sand-carrying business would be decreased. He was a man nearly grown before he found out that his ardor in attempting to kill off all the jay birds was prompted by an "old wife's fable," a myth, one of the many hundred superstitious notions that prevailed among the old-time colored people.

REV. CHARLES T. WALKER AT FORTY YEARS OF AGE.

EARLY RELIGIOUS IMPRESSIONS.

Dr. Walker's first recollection of any religious emotions run back to the period of his early childhood. He remembers how every Sunday night all the servants would gather in the hall of the "Big House," and hold a prayer-meeting with the "old master," a Dr. Samuel Clark, leading the service. He used to go with his mother to these meetings. The fist hymn he ever heard "lined" and sung, *i. e.,* the first hymn that he remembers, was the good, old fashioned hymn beginning,

"When I can read my title clear."

He remembers well the edition then used had these words:

"And hellish darts be hurled,"

Instead of the present rendition, which has these words:

"And fiery darts be hurled."

ELECTING A CHURCH TREASURER.

Dr. Walker and the late Rev. T. J. Hornsby were once invited by a country church in Burke County, Ga., to conduct an election of officers. Bro. Hornsby acted as moderator. The custom of the church, as was true of many others, had been to elect two members to see after the money. One man carried the key, and the other man kept the box. As a rule, the money was counted and the box locked in the presence of the deacons. As a further precaution, the man with the box was not allowed to carry the key. When the time came to elect the treasurer, Dr. Walker explained to the church that it would be best to elect one man as treasurer and make him responsible for both box and key. He told them that the time had passed for them to continue the old custom of electing two men. Some at first were not inclined to favor this new departure. One or two members made speeches against it and said that it would never do, but the majority of those present voted to adopt the suggestion, and accordingly one man was elected treasurer.

Rev. Hornsby, when he declared the election, thinking to add a humorous touch to the situation, said:

"Now, Brother Jenkins is your treasurer. He will have both the box and the key. He can open the box whenever he wants to, and take out what he pleases."

Quick as a flash, an old brother, one of the opposers, rose to his feet and exclaimed: "Dar now; you hear dat! I knowed when we sont fer Brer Hornsby and Dr. Walker dat dere was gwineter be de devil to play here to-day! Dog my cat, I tol' you so, and you wouldn't listen at me, and now hit's too late!"

DR. WALKER'S COMPLEXION.

While in London, on his way to the Holy Land, Dr. Walker, in company with Prof. M. J. Maddox, one of his traveling companions, went to a barber shop to get a shave. Evidently the barber had never seen Negroes before, and was very much astonished. He noticed that Mr. Maddox was several shades lighter as to his color than Dr. Walker. Speaking to the latter about this, the barber asked, "Why is it that you've got so much more complexion than your friend?" He wanted to know, of course, why Dr. Walker was so much darker than Mr. Maddox, and that is the way he put it.

When the barber had nearly finished his work, he said to Dr. Walker, "I'd like to shave you all the time, your hair is so curly." Americans would speak of Dr. Walker's hair as woolly.

THE NEGRO A NOVELTY.

In Heidelberg, Mayence, Cologne and other places, Dr. Walker and Dr. Carter were the observed of all observers. Hundreds of people would gather about them and inspect their clothing and feel their skin.

In Brussels, in a few minutes after they left the station and reached the streets, a crowd of nearly 500 people gathered around and plied them with all sorts of questions. They were asked what was the cause of their blackness; they were asked whether the devil made them black; one man wanted to know if everybody where they came from was black; some wanted to know if their color would wash off; another asked why the palms of their hands were so much lighter than the backs of their hands; and so on almost without limit. When they started down the street, hundreds of children followed them the same as if they were following a circus. The children gladly carried the traveling bags, bundles, and walking canes, umbrellas, etc.—anything to keep up with the strange men. Writing about this to his newspaper at Augusta, Ga., Dr. Walker said:

"In America the Negro is a problem; in Europe he is a novelty."

CHAPTER XX.

APPEARANCE, MANNERS, HABITS.

The Rev. Dr. Walker stands five feet seven inches in his stockings. He weighs 160 pounds. He has a peculiar stoop in his shoulders, not from age, but from a constitutional pliancy of his back-bone, aided by his early habit of incessant reading. In walking, he has a peculiar swaying or swinging gait. Seen from behind, he looks, as he walks with head depressed, bended back, and swaying gait, like an old man. But the expression of his face is singularly and engagingly youthful. A smile plays ever on his countenance. The pleasant, youngish looking face is in marked contrast with his head, which is prematurely gray. Sometimes in referring to his gray hairs, Dr. Walker says that they cannot be signs of hard work or trouble, because he was told by his mother that he had a number of gray hairs in his head in his infancy. His skin is very dark, but there are many very much darker men among the colored people. He never would be taken for a great man, judging from his appearance. Not a large man in stature, without a commanding appearance, he never would be looked at for the second time when one passes him on the street and never would be taken for one of the world's most famous preachers in any large gathering with other distinguished men. It is when he begins to speak that the latent powers of the man are at once apparent to the close student of human nature and the practiced observer of men. When seated, he is like a sea at rest, calm and undisturbed; when on his feet, he is like the sea in action, or like some dictator suddenly sent from another world to correct the faults and foibles of this world.

In manner he is still, to some extent, a rustic. His world-wide travel, his acquaintance with some of the greatest and best of earth and his life in the metropolis of America, have not been able to make much impression upon him. He is an unassimilated man. Great, indeed, are the assimilating powers of the large cities. A youth will go to New York or Boston, awkward, ill-dressed, bashful, and capable of being surprised. After only a few years' absence, he returns to his country home a changed being; his clothes, his accent, his affectations, and his manners are "City-made." His friends do not recognize him at first sight. They do not quite understand his language when he speaks. All his ways are changed. He is another man. It is so with most, but not with all. Some men there are—very few, yet some—who resist effectually or, one might say, unconsciously, and to the last, the assimilating influence of the large cities. They are the oddities, the stared-at, the men of whom anecdotes are told. There is one thing, though, which can be said of them which cannot be said of the other class; there is no affection about them—they do not put on. Everywhere and all the time, Dr. Walker keeps to his Southern training and his Southern style. "I am not a society man," he often says, "and you cannot expect me to be up on etiquette and decorum, and all those fool things." When asked to do the honors at some wedding feast, or sit down and enjoy a sumptuous repast in courses, he has been heard to say, "I am not used to that kind of thing, and I cannot get above my raising."

But it must not be thought that because it is admitted that he is still a rustic in some things that he is at all boorish, unmannered or impolite. No man enjoys the society of people, the intercourse of men, the mutual exchange and interchange of ideas and opinions more than he does, and he would not be likely to mistake finger-bowl for drinking purposes. But his politeness is the politeness of tact and good common sense rather than the politeness of the books and of so-called high society.

In some respects he is exceedingly frank: in others, no man is more reserved. He likes company and likes to talk about the things which interest him most, and there are thousands of living mortals who will testify that they have never found any man in general conversation more interesting or more entertaining than he. In Georgia, where people are always very democratic in their ways, for hours and hours great crowds of men, old and young, have considered it a privilege and an honor to be permitted to stand in some barber shop or drug store or grocery store and listen to Dr. Walker talk. It is very difficult for him to go one square in his home town without being stopped by somebody who really has no other motive than just to hear him talk. When one succeeds in detaining him for a little while, that is usually the signal for others to join the number, and by this process it is not long before Dr. Walker has been intercepted and made to talk. Such a thing would disturb and annoy an ordinary man. But when he is asked if it does not tire him to be worried out by people who merely want to take up his time in talking, he says: "It pleases them, and it doesn't hurt me." He loves a joke—not likes, but loves—and tells a comic story with great glee. His cheerfulness is habitual, and probably he never knew two consecutive hours of melancholy in his life.

He possesses one of the most remarkable memories for names and faces that God has ever given to any man. At one time his membership in Augusta consisted of more than 1,200 persons, and he knew them all by name, and could call their names as soon as he saw them anywhere and at anytime. In Augusta, with a population of 15,000 colored people, more or less, he knows more than half of them by name. The same is true of the people in the country districts in and around Augusta where he has been. He knows the leading men and women in religious, political, and educational circles throughout the state and nation, and can call their names without a moment's hesitation, tell where they are, and what they are doing; in many instances, he knows about their past, about their family connections, about any difficulties they may have had. Of course, this wonderful power of memory must of necessity stand him in good stead in his sermon preparation, in his delivery of sermons, and in his literary work; but it is little short of wonderful how one man could, in the first place, know so much about so many people, and, in the second place, how, if he did know, he could remember it all, even to the smallest detail.

Though humble, meek, modest almost to the point of shyness, there is nothing of obsequiousness about him. It is not his way to bow and scrape and cater to any man, while at the same time he has a becoming respect for the deeds of men and never fails to praise a fellow-mortal for the good that he does. But he hates hypocrisy, he hates cringing. He has never found it necessary to go out of the way to speak with any of the great men of the world with whom he has come in contact or who have attended his meetings in various places from time to time. Sometimes, when he has been told that Mr. So-and-So (a person of some influence) is in the audience, he has replied, "Give him my number, please; if he desires to call, I shall be glad to see him."

He is not what may be called a b okish preacher—that is to say, his sermons do not smell of the lamb. His sermons are, nevertheless, always carefully prepared beforehand, but it is a preparation of prayer, Bible reading and meditation. He goes to the pulpit from his knees, and has often been heard to say, "I know what I am going to say before I come into the pulpit; I know the hymns I am going to sing, the chapter that I am going to read, and I know where the text is to be found." His favorite source of information outside of the Bible is the daily newspaper. He always reads with an eye sigle to the use he can make of the news in his preaching or in his public addresses. In this way, he keeps abreast of the times, and frequently has well-matured opinions on important matters, and many times has spoken of them in public before some other ministers have heard of them. When he enters the pulpit, free from the narrowness that muts come to the man who uses only his Bible commentary, he seems to feel himself under divine compulsion to deliver a message of tanscendent importance to dying men; there is an air about him of a soldier who has a divine commission to fight a great battle for humanity. He speaks directly to the hear., in language all hearts can understand. Humor and pathos, pleading and scorn, impassioned exhortation and cutting sarcasm, all are used in his discourses with tremendous effect.

That he is a man of unpretentious habits and winning manners is evidenced by the great love manifested toward him by the children in the city of Augusta, where he lived so long. Even the children know him and call him by name, and it is an honor without dissimulation, and a tribute without sinister motives that the little children pay when they run in great crowds at sight of the affable preacher, crying as they run, "Howdy, Brer Walker?" "Howdy, Brer Walker?" Many times Dr. Walker will stop and talk with them, ask after their mothers and fathers, and also about their schooling; often he will tell them a little story, and then invite them to church and Sunday school the following Sunday.

CHAPTER XXI.

TRAITS AND CHARACTERISTICS.

One of the leading characteristics that may be mentionel in speaking of Dr. Walker's traits is this: He is accustomed to bear injuries and insults with great patience and forbearance. All the great men of earth from the time of Christ to the present day have been subjected to calumny, abuse, contumely, and misrepresentation in some form or other. George Washington, during his second administration, was called a traitor, because he would not go to war with England. Epithets were ap-applied to him which would hardly have been applied to a Nero, a notorious defaulter, or a common pickpocket. Abraham Lincoln was called a poltroon, a hypocrite, because he was deliberate, painstaking and cautious about issuing the Emancipation Proclamation. Horace Greeley, who, with his paper, the New York Tribune, did more than any other individual in America to bring about the abolition of slavery, was most bitterly denounced by the American people, because he dared to go on the bond of Jefferson Davis, the animosity and vituperation having reached their climax in his campaign against Grant for the presidency. Henry Ward Beecher, who was without a peer in the American pulpit, was hounded down by the venomous tongue of slander and dragged into court on an infamous charge. Dwight L. Moody had his bitter with his sweet. On his first evangelistic campaign in

Europe the papers boldly asserted that he was in the employ of P. T. Barnum, the great show man, and that he was making thousands for his own use out of a credulous public. His issuing of the "Moody and Sankey Hymn Book" was declared to be a huge money-making venture, and people were advised not to purchase it. The great and good William McKinley, the patient, praying President, was most bitterly assailed, his motives most bitterly impunged, and he was called "the puppet president," "the tool," "the manakin." President Roosevelt has said that the man who has not made mistakes is the man who has not done anything. It might be said with equal truth that the man who has not been assailed and opposed is the man who has not done anything. How could Dr. Walker escape? A man's character is not evinced by the manner in which he is slandered and abused and traduced, nevertheless; but a man's character is shown by the manner in which he accepts misrepresentation and abuse and slander. Dr. Walker has the courage which faces difficulties, braves rebuke and contumely, is not afraid of harsh names and ugly epithets; the courage that can look danger and persecution in the face and not shrink before them, brave before ridicule not less than before threatening; the rare courage which in the discharge of duty is not afraid of what men shall say. Though he likes popularity—and who does not?—yet no consideration of public favor can frighten him from speaking his mind, from saying what he believes to be true, from saying what he believes that the people ought to hear. Such courage is of a higher order than an animal instinct, more difficult to maintain, and more trying to a sensitive soul. The bravery that bears misunderstanding is more radical than the bravery that returns blows or fights battles. He has repeatedly said that he has tried to make these words the motto of his life: "I am determined never to be guilty of ingratitude; never to desert a friend; never to strike back at an enemy." I have known Dr. Walker intimately for more than twenty years. I have eaten with him, slept with him, traveled with him, prayed with him, worked with him, played with him; I have known some of the indignities, which have been heaped upon him, and some of the hard things, which he has been called upon to bear; and I truly believe that, in his dealings with those who have wronged him, as well as in his dealings with humanity in general, he is the most Christlike man I ever knew. He comes nearer fulfilling in his own life and person the divine injunction, "Love your enemies; do good to them that despitefully use you," than any man of my extended acquaintance. Perhaps the following admonition and advice sent to me by him in a letter at a time of great trial in my own life, will better show his character on this point than anything I could say. Here is what he said: "You must expect that some will misrepresent both your conduct and your motives. You must expect that your best efforts will be thwarted by the folly or wickedness of those whom you propose to serve. Be it so. Spend no time or strength in unavailing regrets. Spend no time or strength in repelling the attempted injury. Go forward in the way of duty. Let your uniform good conduct be your defence. Time is the great corrector. Your conduct will one day be seen in its true light. If not, God always sees it in its true light, and will reward every man according to his works." These were noble words from a noble soul. God does not call his ministers to seats of ease, nor yet to the enjoyment of undisturbed comforts. Their duties are of such a nature and their environment is so peculiar that such a call in this life is impossible. Indeed, it often happens that the more faithful a minister is to his divine vocation, the more bitter will be the cup he is called upon to drain. Had it been otherwise, the name of many a noble man of God, enshrined in the hearts of millions of the race, would never have been heard beyond his parish boundaries. In every church, even those conducted on sound principles, there are a few polyphagous members whom no gospel preacher can supply. They are ever restive, ever seeking after novelties, ever grumbling, ever finding fault. Dr. Walker has met people of this class in his pastoral work, and he has won them by love and kindness. He has proved in this way that the word of the Master is true, "Love your enemies, bless them that curse you, do good to them that hate you, and pray for them which despitefully use you and persecute you; that ye may be the children of your Father which is in heaven."

Humility is also a distinguishing trait in the character of Dr. Walker. The beauty of humility is delightfully displayed in him, and its influence is extensively felt and acknowledged. Hence, arise the love and respect so generally entertained for him. It has been remarked that scarcely any person could be in his presence for an hour without loving him. There has always been about him a beautiful unmindfulness of himself while engaged in his life-work. In this respect he is different from many, for self-consciousness and solicitous guardianship over their own rights and honors characterize mankind in general. At the recent meeting in Mt. Olivet Baptist Church, held to protest against his returning to labor with his old church at Augusta, one of the most prominent young men of the church spoke in substance as follows: "I want to confess something here that I have never before told anybody, not even Dr. Walker. Dr. Walker has done more to take false pride out of me than any man living. The other day I was going down Broadway, and I passed Dr. Walker. I stopped and shook his hand, and being somewhat in a hurry, kept on down the street. Shortly after I had passed him I met a young man whom I knew well, but he wasn't well dressed—in fact, he was dressed very shabbily—and I didn't want to speak to him. I turned my head away from him, so as to keep from speaking. I looked back to see if Dr. Walker would speak to him. Dr. Walker stopped and shook that young man's hand and stood up in Broadway, with all the people going by, to talk with him, and Dr. Walker seemed just as glad to see him as he had been to see me. I learned a lesson from that scene that I will never forget."

Dr. Walker, also, has a responsive feeling of gratitude for mercies and favors received. This spirit is always associated with true humility; for in proportion to the Christian's sense of his own unworthiness, is his thankfulness for those supplies which he forfeited by his rebellion. Dr. Walker views every blessing, both temporal and spiritual, as coming to him immediately from the hand of God through the mediation of Jesus Christ.

Christian charity pre-eminently adorns the character of Dr. Walker. The love which glows in Dr. Walker's heart was evidently enkindled by the Holy Ghost and has produced a cordial feeling of good-will toward all men, of whatever grade or country, of whatever party or sect. While he is an ardent and uncompromising Baptist, his treatment of other Christian denominations is fraternal and appreciative; his spirit is broad and catholic; there is nothing ultra-sectarian in his make-up. Those who love him because of this are found in the Methodist church, the Congregational church, the Presbyterian church, the Episcopalian church, the Baptist church, and in all churches and in no churches. He has a tender fellow-feeling for the poor and afflicted, and has many times denied himself lawful gratifications for their sake. He has cheerfully submitted to any service, and thought nothing too low or too mean, in which to engage, if thereby he could benefit either the souls or bodies of men.

There are other features which ought to be mentioned. Clearness of vision, capacity for hard work and quick decisions, executive force, the ability to guide the thoughts and energies of other men into the same channel as his own, and thus unite their force with his, and his mastery of details, are conspicuous elements in his character.

Charles T. Walker has his faults, like other men. These are not to be overlooked, and I mention this fact, in closing this chapter, in order to say that Charles T. Walker is not a perfect man. A perfect man has not trod this planet since Christ left it. It is said of Charles Lamb, that he liked his friends, not in spite of their faults, but faults and all. And Charles Lamb was no less right than kind. The errors of a true man are not discreditable to him, for his errors spring from the same source as his excellencies. Moreover, it is very difficult to judge character. Generally speaking, those who are familiar with a man are blind to his faults, and those who are not intimate are blind to his virtues. Still, in summing up the traits and characteristics of Dr. Walker, it may be truthfully said that he is no ordinary man, and that one would be compelled to search among sinful mortals many and many a day before he would find one man who, in all respects, possesses more of the traits of genuine honor, manhood and sterling worth than does the present pastor of the Mount Olivet Baptist Church, New York City.

CHAPTER XXII.

CONCLUSION.

Of the countless gifts which God bestows upon man, the rarest, the most divine, is an ability to take supreme interest in human welfare. If any pious soul will accurately ascertain what it is in the character of the Man Christ Jesus, the contemplation of which fills his heart with rapture and his eyes with tears, that pious soul will know what is here meant by the expression "supreme interest in human welfare." Most of us, alarmed at the dangers which beset our lives, distracted with cares, blinded with desires to secure our own safety, are absorbed in schemes of personal advantage. Only a few men go apart, ascend the heights, survey the scene with serene, unselfish eye, and make discoveries which those engaged in their own selfish pursuits could never arrive at. But for such, the race of mankind would long ago have extirpated itself in its mad, blind strife. But for such, it never would have been discovered that no individual can be safe in welfare while any other individual is not.

In summing up the life story of Dr. Walker, I ask myself what it is that has given this man of God such a place in the affection, regard and sincere esteem of those who know and love and honor him. Is it mere intellectual ability? Great as is his intellectual strength, there are many men in his same calling of greater intellect, but they are not known and loved as he is. Is it official station? He holds no office except that of an humble minister of the gospel. Is it wealth? Dr. Walker is a poor man. In his case, I believe that the secret lies in active Christian charity, or what might be called the magnetism of simple goodness. I need not say that Dr. Walker's heart is as large as his brain—that love for humanity is an inwrought element of his nature. It is manifested in a kindness and regard that keep a silent record in many hearts; in a hand ever open and ready to help; in one of the kindest faces ever worn by man, the expression of which is

"A meeting of gentle lights without a name."

How wide, how manifold is the circle of interests which he has touched! How many, many minds has he instructed with practical wisdom! How many lives has he stimulated to wholesome energy! How many young men greatfully acknowledge him as their teacher and guide! How many aged people, how many orphans have looked up to him for succor! How many precious souls have been saved for truth, for righteousness, for God! His pen never idle, his lips never still his feet never weary, what a blessing he has been to his day and generation! In his eyes, the noblest career is that which is given up to others' wants. The successful life is that which is worn out in conflict with wrong and woe. The only ambition worth following is the ambition to alleviate human misery and leave the world better—a little better for one's having lived in it.

And this, verily, is the greatness which the world at last acknowledges, confesses, honors—the greatness of goodness. Those who read this story of Dr. Walker's life ought, therefore, to be encouraged, not discouraged, because the greatness of goodness is a communicable power for the goodness of mankind and, unlike intellectual power, unlike official station, unlike wealth, may be attained by all. Let the reader, then, drink from this story inspiration for his best endeavors, while he thanks God that the achievement in Dr. Walker's case has been so large and so effective. The real forces of the world are not those which science chiefly delights to celebrate, but those other inward spiritual forces, such as righteousness, justice and truth, which lie behind the more visible energies, giving them all the real power that they possess, and guiding them, not blindly, but intelligently, to rational and beneficent ends.

UNIVERSITAS
The Ellen Clarke Bertrand Library
18
46
BUCNELLENSIS